LIFE SERIES

Windows of Heaven

Level 8
Seventh-day Adventist Readers

Patricia A. Habada

Sally J. McMillan

Blossom Engen

Frances Blahovich

Mitzi J. Smith

Acknowledgments

Grateful acknowledgment is made to the following:

Ginn and Company for assistance in the preparation of this book; and to Rosly Walter, Ginn staff editor, for guidance.

Reading steering committee members: Marion Hartlein, chairman; Patricia Habada, secretary; Frances Clark, Southwestern Union; Erna Hauck, Columbia Union College; Sandra Herndon, Northeastern Conference; Elizabeth Hudak, Florida Conference; Erma Lee, North Pacific Union; Norwida Marshall, Southern Union; Lorraine Miller, Oregon Conference; Joyce Morse, Southern California Conference; Esther Novak, Wisconsin Conference; Desmond Rice, Southern College; Aleene Schaeffer, Union College; George Unger, Canadian Union.

Canadian consultants: Herbert Penney-Flynn, Newfoundland; Frances Schander, Saskatchewan; George Unger, Ontario.

Special consultants: Margaret Hafner, New York; Betty McCune, Loma Linda University; Millie Youngberg, Andrews University.

Grateful acknowledgment is made to the following publishers, authors, and agents for permission to use and adapt copyrighted materials:

Clyde Robert Bulla for "The Invitation."

E. P. Dutton for the adaptation of "Girls Can Be Anything" by Norma Klein. Text copyright © 1973 by Norma Klein. Reprinted by permission of the publisher, E. P. Dutton, a division of New American Library.

Aileen Fisher for "Cat Bath" by Aileen Fisher. Used by permission of the author.

Grosset & Dunlap for "Rhyme" by Elizabeth Coatsworth. Reprinted by permission of Grosset & Dunlap from *The Sparrow Bush* by Elizabeth Coatsworth, copyright © 1966 by Grosset & Dunlap, Inc.

Margaret Haun for the adaptation of her story, "The Rescue."

Arthur Honeyman for his story, "Sam and His Cart" from the book *Sam and His Cart*. Copyright © 1980 by Arthur Honeyman. Used by permission of Arthur Honeyman.

Edith Thatcher Hurd for her story, "Bears Aren't Everywhere."

Instructor Publications for "Kangaroo Ride" by Elaine V. Emans. Reprinted from *Poetry Place Anthology*. Copyright © 1983 by the Instructor Publications, Inc. Used by permission.

Schroer Lee for the adaptation of the story "Well, Why Didn't You Say So?" by Jo Anne Wold. Copyright 1975 by Jo Anne Wold.

Katherine Q. Morton for the adaptation of her story, "Special Visitors."

G.P. Putnam's Sons for "The Island" by Dorothy Aldis reprinted by permission of G.P. Putnam's Sons. From *All Together* by Dorothy Aldis, copyright © 1925, 1952, copyright renewed 1953, 1967 by Dorothy Aldis.

Marian Reiner for "Trees" from *The Little Hill* Poems and Pictures by Harry Behn. Copyright © 1949 by Harry Behn, renewed 1977 by Alice L. Behn. Reprinted by permission of Marian Reiner.

Cynthia Stone Richmond for "Finding the Way" adapted from "Fun for Maria" by Cynthia Stone Richmond.

Russell & Volkening, Inc. for "I Like Old Clothes" by Mary Ann Hoberman. Reprinted by permission of Russell & Volkening, Inc. as agents for the author. Copyright © 1976 by Mary Ann Hoberman.

Every effort has been made to trace the ownership of all copyrighted material in this book and to obtain permission for its use.

Illustrations and photographs were provided by the following:

Angela Moizio Ackerman (88-98, 220-235); Lois Axeman (153-162); Mary Bausman (30-43); Mark Bellerose (78-83); Dave Blanchette (45, 164); Rick Cooley (63-69); Ray Cruz (133-142); Faith Cushing (112); John DeCindas (198-203); E. R. Degginger (122-123); Bill Denison (186-187); Jeffrey Dever (99-102, 163, 168-174); Jack Freas (112); Sasha Georgevitch (246-281); Nathan Greene (236); M. Habicht/TAURUS PHOTOS, INC. (121); Trina Hyman (70-77); Susan Jeffers (57-62); Annie Lunsford (19-28); Alan Mardon (103-111); M. Mittelmann/TAURUS PHOTOS, INC. (121); Pat Morrison (8-18, 29); Carol L. Mullin (113-120); NASA (193, 195); Tony Rao (183); Mary Rumford (143-152, 245); Paul Salmon (128-132, 214-219, 237-243); Roz Schanzer (204); Dan Siculan (57-61); Richard Steadham (208-213, 244); George Ulrich (44, 125, 165, 204, 205).

The unit introduction pages were designed by Gregory Fosella Associates. Cover design by Dennis Feree. Cover photo by Camerique. Dever Designs provided consultation services in art and design.

Contents

Unit 6 ONCE THERE WAS

BOOK-LENGTH STORY

GLOSSARY   **282**

6

Lost and Found

7

TURN RIGHT AT THE TREE

It was hot in the car even with all the windows open. Judy and her brother Gus sat in the back seat. Mother and Father sat in front. They were looking at a map. The Christopher family was on its way to the church picnic.

That is, they hoped they were on their
way.

"I'm hungry," said Gus.

"We're lost," said Judy.

"I'm afraid so," said Mrs. Christopher.

10

Mr. Christopher stopped the car. He said, "Let's take another look at Mr. Ross's map."

"That's the fence," said Mr. Christopher. They saw it on the map. They looked out the back window at the fence they had passed.

"We turned right at the fence on that road," said Mrs. Christopher. They saw the road on the map.

"That's the tree where we turned left," said Judy. Again they saw the tree on the map and out the window.

"Here's the barn," said Gus. There it was on the map and out the window.

"Here we are," said Mr. Christopher.

"But where is the park?" asked Gus. The park was on the map all right, but they did not see it out the window.

11

"Something's wrong somewhere," said Mr. Christopher.

"It must be the map that's wrong," said Mrs. Christopher. "We followed it exactly."

"What do we do now?" Judy asked.

"We're going back to the highway," said Mr. Christopher as he started the car.

"We're going to miss the softball game," said Judy.

"I'm hungry," said Gus.

Just as they reached the highway, Judy saw a man on horseback, riding across the field.

"Stop the car, Daddy," said Judy. "Let's ask that man."

"Maybe he knows where the park is," said Gus.

So they stopped and waited for the man to reach them.

"Hello there," said Mr. Christopher to the man. "We seem to be lost. Can you tell us how to get to Pine Park?"

The man smiled and said, "You're not too far off. See that tree back there?" It was the one where they had turned left. "Well, go back to the tree and turn right. Then just keep going until you see a barn. At the barn you turn left. You'll see the park right in front of you," he said.

"Thank you," said Mr. Christopher.

They turned around and went back to the tree.

"This is where the map is wrong," said Mrs. Christopher.

"Yes," said Judy. "You turn right at the tree—not left."

They turned right. They saw a barn. It looked just like the barn they had passed before. They turned left.

"There's the park!" said Gus.

"And there's Mr. Ross!" said Judy.

"Am I glad to see you people," said Mr. Ross. He looked very upset. The Christophers got out of their car.

"Where is everyone?" asked Gus.

"I don't know," said Mr. Ross. "It looks like no one is coming. I gave maps to . . . ."

"But the map was wrong," said Judy.

"What?" said Mr. Ross. "Are you sure?"

"Here," said Mr. Christopher, "we'll show you." They all looked at the map together.

"So that's why no one's here," said Mr. Ross. "I'd better hurry back to that tree."

"I'll come with you," said Mr. Christopher.

"Wait, Daddy, I've got an idea," Judy said as she ran over to the car. She got a box from the back seat.

"I brought along some paper and pens," she said. She opened the box and took out a sheet of paper. "I can make a sign."

"Use the red pen," said Gus.

"O.K.," said Judy and before you could say Pine Park, she had made a sign. The sign said: TURN RIGHT, NOT LEFT.

"Good thinking," said Mr. Ross.

"We can put the sign on the tree," said Mr. Christopher.

Mr. Ross and Mr. Christopher drove back to the tree to put up Judy's sign. Judy, Gus, and their mother took the things they had brought for the picnic out of the car. There were blankets. Gus had a ball and bat. Judy had a jump rope. There were two big picnic baskets with sandwiches, baked beans, salad, and gingerbread.

"I'm so hungry," said Gus as he took one basket out of the car.

"Me, too," said Judy as she put down the other one.

"It won't be long now," said Mother.

And it wasn't long before Gus saw the first car turn left at the barn. He waved. He called Judy and they both waved. Then another car came and another and another. The picnic had begun.

Why Didn't You Say So?

Willie was gone!

John looked under the picnic table. He looked inside the garage. He called and whistled. Finally John said, "I wonder where Willie went?"

No one knew. Not his mother. Not his father.

"You go look for Willie," his mother said.

So John went walking, walking, until he
came to a man raking apple leaves.

"Have you seen Willie?" John asked.

"What does he look like?" asked the man.

"He is mostly brown," John answered.

"No. I haven't seen him," the man said,
and he went on raking leaves.

John passed the apple trees. Trees, trees,
row upon row. But no Willie.

John kept on walking. Soon he saw three girls, all with pigtails, all roller-skating in a driveway.

"Have you seen Willie?" John called.

"What does he look like?" one girl asked.

"He is mostly brown. And he has a long tail with white on it."

"Oh, no!" the girls answered together. "We haven't seen Willie."

John kept on walking. It wasn't long before he saw the ice cream woman in her truck.

"Hello," John called. "Have you seen Willie?"

"Peach is the special today," the ice cream woman answered, leaning out of the truck window.

"No, no," John said. "I don't want ice cream. I want Willie. Have you seen him?"

"Oh, no," the woman said as she rang her bell.

"Are you sure?" John asked. "You don't even know what he looks like."

"Well, what does he look like?"

"He is mostly brown. And he has a long tail with white on it. And he has one blue eye and one brown eye."

"I haven't seen Willie," the ice cream woman said, and she drove away.

John kept on walking until he came to a small house among tall trees. An old lady with a red kerchief on her head was feeding the birds.

"Hello," John called. "Have you seen Willie?"

"Willie? Willie?" the old lady asked. "What does Willie look like?"

"He's mostly brown. And he has a long tail with white on it. One blue eye and one brown eye. And he is this tall," John said, placing his hand at his waist.

"Oh, no," the old lady said. "I haven't seen him." She shook her head sadly.

John's feet dragged. Where, oh! where, had Willie gone?

There was one more place to go. John ran to the service station. If Willie wasn't there, then he was gone forever.

The service station man was putting gas in a car.

"Have you seen Willie?" John asked.

"What does Willie look like?" the service station man wanted to know.

John took a deep breath. "He is mostly brown. And he has a long tail with white on it. One blue eye and one brown eye. About this tall, and he has a red collar."

"Nope," the service station man said. "I haven't seen him. I haven't seen him at all." He said it two times, just to make sure.

John turned to go home. Willie, Willie, where are you? he wondered.

John came to the small house among the tall trees. The old lady who had been feeding the birds poked her head out of the window. Her red kerchief waved in the wind.

"Did you find your pony?" she called.

"My pony! I'm not looking for a pony," John shouted. "I'm looking for my dog."

"Your dog? My, oh my! Why didn't you say so?" the old lady said.

Pretty soon he saw the ice cream truck. The ice cream woman stopped and called, "Did you find your goat?"

"My goat! I'm not looking for a goat," John said. "I'm looking for my dog."

"Your dog!" the ice cream woman said, and rang her bell. "Why in the world didn't you say so?"

When John passed the girls with roller skates, they were sitting under a tree.

"Did you find your squirrel?" they all called out together.

"My squirrel! I'm not looking for a squirrel. I'm looking for my D-O-G," and he spelled it out for them, just like that.

The girls laughed and asked, "Well, why didn't you say so?"

Finally John was back where he'd started. The man raking leaves was still at work.

"Did you find your cat?" he asked.

"My cat! I'm not looking for a cat. I am looking for my dog. D-O-G!" John said that as loudly as he could.

The man leaned on his rake and laughed. "A dog! A D-O-G! Well, why didn't you say so? Is he brown, with a long tail with white on it? With one blue eye and one brown eye? About this tall, and does he have a red collar?"

"Yes!" John shouted. "That's Willie!"

"Oh? I found a dog like that, and I put him in my garage," the man said.

"Well, why didn't you say so?" John wanted to know.

"You didn't ask," the man said.

28

Cat Bath

After she eats,
my purry friend
washes herself
from end to end,

Washes her face,
her ears, her paws,
washes the pink
between her claws.

I watch, and think
it's better by far
to splash in a tub
with soap in a bar

And washcloth in hand
and towel on the rung
than have to do all
that work *by tongue*.

—*Aileen Fisher*

RING AROUND THE ROSES

1. At Miss Anna's House

Springtime had come, and with it came warm sunny days. Flowers pushed their way up through the ground. On the trees new leaves nodded in the breeze.

Every day after school, Emily, Toni, and Suzie walked to Miss Anna's house. Miss Anna lived down the block from school. She was their baby-sitter and their friend.

"Let's race," said Toni.

"O.K.," said Suzie.

"On your mark," said Emily.

"Get set," said Suzie.

"Go!" said Toni. And they were off.

"I won," said Suzie.

"You always win," said Toni who was the baby.

"No, I don't, Toni," said Suzie who was in the middle.

"One day, you'll be faster than both of us," said Emily who was older than the other two.

"I'm in the backyard, children," Miss Anna called over the fence.

They went around to the backyard.

"Guess what?" said Miss Anna in her happy voice. "Today we're going to make a garden. Put your things down on the steps. The fruit is on the table."

Miss Anna always had fruit ready for the children.

They put their things down and got their fruit. Then they sat down on the steps next to Miss Anna. She gave each of them a big hug.

"What a beautiful day," said Miss Anna.

Preparing the Ground

Miss Anna took some little packs out of her pockets. Each pack had a picture on it. She passed them out, one pack for each.

"These are your seeds," said Miss Anna.

"I have corn," said Toni.

"Mine are beans," said Emily.

"I have peas," Suzie said.

"And I have the cabbage plants," said Miss Anna.

"Corn, peas, cabbages, and beans. Our garden will be all yellows and greens," she said, making a little song. Then she laughed and Emily, Toni, and Suzie laughed too. Miss Anna always made them laugh.

"Leave your seeds here on the steps," said Miss Anna. "First, we have to prepare the ground." She gave each one a strong stick.

33

"Now, let's make a line. Take your sticks and make a row from here to here," Miss Anna said. She showed them where. "Now dig in and keep going back and forth until your row is really deep."

The children started working.

"Like this?" asked Toni.

Miss Anna came over and looked. "A little more," said Miss Anna.

"Like this?" asked Emily.

"A little more," said Miss Anna.

"How about this?" asked Suzie.

"Just right," said Miss Anna.

Planting the Seeds

"Now for the seeds," said Miss Anna. The children started to go get their seed packages.

"Wait!" said Miss Anna. "First we have to make holes for the seeds. Dig in with your stick and turn it around and around like this." She showed them how.

"One at a time, now and not too close. That's good," she said, looking at their work.

"Now the seeds," said Toni.

"Right," said Miss Anna, "drop a few in at a time." They did.

"Now we cover them," said Emily.

"Right," said Miss Anna.

When they had finished, Miss Anna said, "Now put your stick in the ground at the end of your row." She showed them how. Then she said, "Take your pack and push it down onto the top of the stick."

"All done," said Suzie.

"All done," said the others. The vegetable garden was planted.

2. Two Surprises

The next day, Emily, Suzie, and Toni could hardly wait to get out of school. They ran all the way to Miss Anna's house and there she was on the front steps.

"There you are," she said, giving them a big hug. The girls got their fruit and sat down with Miss Anna.

"How's our garden?" asked Emily after she took a bite.

"Just fine," said Miss Anna. "Today I thought we could plant flowers in the front yard, but I'm too busy."

"O-h-h-h," said Toni.

"I know," said Miss Anna. "But I have to get the house ready."

"Ready for what?" asked Toni.

"For two visitors who are coming to talk at the church," Miss Anna told them. "They will stay with me."

"Can we help you?" asked Suzie.

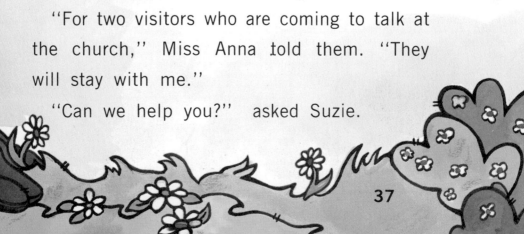

"That's really nice of you, Suzie, but I'll be able to do it," answered Miss Anna. "I want you and Toni and Emily to play outside today. That would help me more than anything."

Then Miss Anna made another word song. It went like this: "Today you have a good time and play. We'll plant our flowers another day." She laughed and the girls laughed with her.

Miss Anna went back into the house. Toni, Emily, and Suzie went to the backyard to see the vegetable garden. They were so proud of it.

Then they decided to play hide-and-seek. Just as they were going back into the front yard, they saw something on the ground. Emily picked it up.

"It's a seed package," she said.

"But it doesn't have a picture like the others," said Toni.

"It must be flower seeds," said Suzie.

"Yes," said Emily. "Maybe flower seeds come in this kind of package."

"I wish we could plant them," said Toni.

"Me, too," said Suzie.

"Why don't we?" said Emily. "We could surprise Miss Anna."

The First Surprise

They decided to do just that. Very quietly, they found a stick. Then they worked in a circle around the roses and they planted the seeds. When they were all done, they called Miss Anna. She came out of the house.

"Look, Miss Anna," they said proudly. "We've planted flowers for you."

"That's great," said Miss Anna. "That's exactly where I wanted to plant the flowers. Thank you, children." She smiled as she gave them another big hug.

The days came and went. The Adventist workers came and the children got to know them. They told the children stories of Adventists in faraway lands. They showed them pictures too.

Every day Emily, Suzie, Toni, and Miss Anna looked at their gardens—the vegetable garden in the backyard and the flower garden in the front yard. They waited and watched for the first sign of green.

The Second Surprise

One day when the children reached Miss Anna's house, she was standing by the roses. Miss Anna had a funny look on her face.

"Miss Anna," said Emily, "what's wrong?"

"Look!" said Miss Anna. They looked at the ground by the roses.

"Our flowers!" said Toni.

"They've come out," said Suzie. The girls got down closer to see the little green leaves.

"But they're not flowers," said Miss Anna. "They're radishes."

"Radishes?" asked Emily.

"Radishes," said Miss Anna.

"Oh, dear," said Emily, remembering the seed pack without pictures.

"Oh, Miss Anna," said Emily, "we planted the wrong ones."

"We're sorry. We're so sorry, Miss Anna," they said again.

"Sorry? What for?" Miss Anna said laughing. She took their hands and they made a circle. Laughing together, they skipped around the roses while Miss Anna sang a new song.

"Ring around the roses,
Radishes in a row.
Ring around the roses,
Radishes will grow."

Riddles

I help people find their way.
I show where streets go.
I show parks and buildings.
I am _____ .

I drive a truck.
I stop for children.
They buy ice cream from me.
I am _____ .

Miss Anna likes me.
I grow on a bush.
I can be red or yellow.
I am a _____ .

I wear a red collar.
I have a long tail.
A man put me in his garage.
I am _____ .

Yes or No

Explain your answers.

1. Can you mail a rose in an envelope?
2. If you wish on a rosebush, will your wish come true?
3. Does a surprise make you happy?
4. Do radishes grow above the ground?
5. Is a map like a picture?
6. If you plant brown seeds, will beans grow?
7. Do people always eat at a picnic?
8. Do dogs like to get lost?
9. Is a garage a good place to keep radishes?

Building Sentences

Choose a picture or word for each stage of the rocket to make a sentence. Make your sentence take off by adding more words.

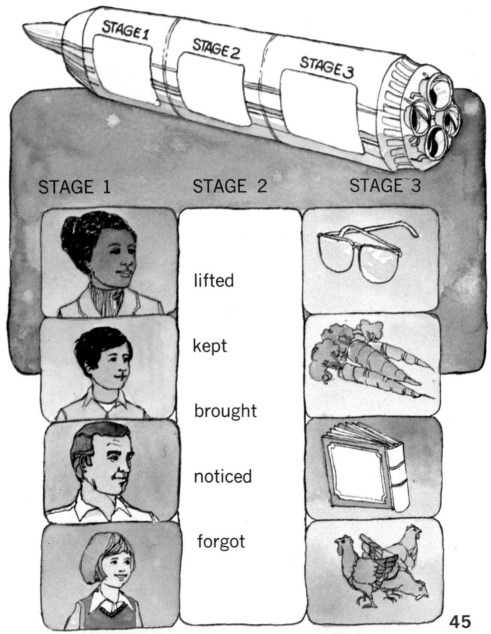

STAGE 1   STAGE 2   STAGE 3

lifted

kept

brought

noticed

forgot

45

Very Special Friends

47

Speck

Spring was coming to Tait Adventist School. On the new highway big trucks went by the school all day. And new red, green, and yellow signals were ready at the school crossing. The girls and boys in Miss Day's class were talking about them.

"I'm sure you know how to obey the new signals, don't you?" Miss Day asked.

Mark Zapella answered. "First we check the lights. Green, red, or yellow. We know about them. But now we watch for the new signal that says W-A-L-K. Then we obey it and go across the highway, and we stay inside the crosswalk lines."

Everyone nodded but Ben. He was thinking about his dog, Speck.

Ann Dines added something. "My mother meets me every day after school. She doesn't want me to cross the highway without her."

"Why not?" Mark asked. "All we have to do is obey the new signals."

The children talked and Miss Day listened. Finally she asked Ben a question, "What do you think about obeying signals?"

Ben said, "I was thinking about my dog, Speck. He obeys."

Speck was Ben's new Springer Spaniel. His coat was white with black specks in it. He could do tricks. He could catch a ball. He could stand on his hind legs and beg. He knew how to obey signals.

"How many signals can Speck obey?" Miss Day asked.

Ben named them. "When my Dad says 'Come,' Speck comes. When Dad says 'Heel,' Speck walks along beside him. He says 'Stay!' and Speck stays where he is until Dad tells him to move. Oh, Speck obeys signals all right."

Ann asked another question, "Does he obey you?"

"Yes," Ben said. "I'm his master now, and he's just learned how to fetch."

"How does he fetch?" asked Ann.

"Well, my baby sister creeps everywhere now. Sometimes she goes too far away. I call Speck and point to the baby. I say 'Fetch!' and Speck races to her. He pulls at her dress with his teeth. He doesn't rip her dress. He never bites her. He just pulls her back to me. Then I give him a special biscuit. That special biscuit makes him happy and . . ."

Mark Zapella asked, "Can you bring Speck to school so we can see him fetch?"

Ben said, "I can't bring my baby sister too, but I could bring her doll and show you. That's how I trained Speck. He learned to fetch with the doll."

"May I bring my little sister to watch Speck?" Ann Dines asked. "Little Jenny needs to learn to obey too."

Ben did bring Speck to school one afternoon, and Ann brought Little Jenny for this special time.

Speck obeyed every command that Ben gave him.

"Fetch!" Ben commanded. He pointed to the doll. All the children watched Speck. Jenny watched too.

Speck skidded across the schoolroom floor to the doll. He grabbed her dress with his teeth. With great care he pulled her back to his master.

Jenny laughed and laughed.

After school Ben took Speck out to the school crosswalk near the new signals. His father was going to meet them there.

"Sit!" Ben commanded, and Speck obeyed. He sat very upright, close to his master's feet. Ben watched the highway for his father's truck. It was time for it to come.

Ann Dines came out with Jenny to wait for their mother.

"Sit, stay, fetch!" Jenny commanded Speck, but the dog did not move.

Ben wished the truck would come. Jenny was a pest.

Then Ben heard a horn. His father's truck was slowly moving nearer the crosswalk.

Jenny began to jump up and down. "Over there ! Over there ! There's Mommy !"

Across the highway at the other end of the crosswalk Mrs. Dines was waiting. The signal light was red, and Jenny's mother was signaling her to wait with Ann.

The truck was rolling closer. Jenny did not see the truck or the red light or her mother's signaling. Before Ann could stop her, Jenny darted out into the crosswalk.

Ben saw her. He bent down and pointed to Jenny. "FETCH HER !" he commanded.

In one bound Speck had Jenny by her shirt. He gave a quick hard pull, and Jenny landed on the curb again. She was screaming, but she was safe.

The truck had stopped. The brakes had held. Ben's father jumped out of the truck and hurried over to the children.

Ann helped Jenny stand up, and she put her arms around her little sister. Jenny stopped screaming and watched Ben and Speck.

Ben was patting Speck. "Good dog, good dog," he kept saying as he pulled out a special biscuit. "Sit!" he commanded. "Stay!" Speck obeyed, and Ben gave him the biscuit.

Now the crosswalk signal said W-A-L-K. Mrs. Dines hurried across the highway. "Oh, Jenny!" she cried. "That dog saved you."

Speck just sat upright beside his master and chewed his biscuit.

Roady Roadrunner and Yoshi

Roady Roadrunner lived in the high desert. Roady's house was a prickly bush by the side of the road. Yoshi lived in the high desert too. Every morning on her way to school Yoshi passed Roady's house, and Roady always ran out of the bush to greet her.

Roady had strong legs for running, and a long strong tail. The tail stayed out straight behind her when she ran. When she stopped running, her tail would stand straight up. It was like a brake. It helped Roady to make a quick stop.

One morning when Roady ran to meet Yoshi, she sang a strange song. It sounded a little like a cuckoo, because Roady belonged to the cuckoo family. She sang the song, and then she cocked her head.

Yoshi stood and looked at her. "If I could run as fast as you run," she said, "I could be on time for school. I am late every day."

Roady ran ahead of Yoshi and made a quick stop at a fork in the road. Roady braked her run with her strong tail. Then she stood there, waiting for Yoshi.

At the fork one road went on in a straight line to the school. It was the best way to go. It was the shorter way.

Yoshi did not go the shorter way. On that road a big black dog lived. It barked at her. It was very strong, and one day it had pushed her down. She was afraid of it.

The other road was longer. Yoshi went that way to school. She hurried. Sometimes she ran. But she was always late for school because that way took longer.

Her teacher, Mr. Pine, always looked upset when she came in late. Today he said, "Yoshi, you are late again! Please promise to be on time tomorrow. Why is it that you are always late?"

Yoshi stood with her head down and could not answer. If she told about the dog, the children would laugh at her.

At closing time Mr. Pine said, "Promise to be on time tomorrow, Yoshi. Please try."

"I will try," she said softly. "I promise."

The next morning Roady Roadrunner did not run out to meet Yoshi. She heard a whirring buz-z-z-z in the bush. It sounded like a rattlesnake.

Yoshi looked behind the bush. There was Roady, and there was a small rattlesnake. It was ready to strike Roady!

But Roady did not run away on her strong fast legs. She ran straight at the little snake. The snake missed its strike, and Roady pecked at its head. Then Roady jumped back and stopped where the snake could not strike her. Roady was ready to run at it again.

Roady was in danger. She was a brown bird, all alone. She did not run away, but the snake did. It found a rock and crawled under it.

Yoshi ran back to the road, but Roady was there first. Roady cocked her head and gave Yoshi her greeting.

Yoshi bowed. "You are a brave bird," she said. "You are really strong."

Then she started to go on to school.

Roady ran ahead to the fork of the road. Roady braked her tail and looked at Yoshi and sang her cooing song.

"Are you telling me not to be afraid?" Yoshi asked the bird as she came to the place where the road forked.

She looked down the shorter road to the school and saw the dog lying there. She looked at Roady and remembered how bravely she had faced the snake.

Yoshi took a big breath. "I can look after myself too," she said. "Jesus will help me." And she took the shorter way.

She walked right by the dog. It growled a little, but she did not stop. The dog did not bark. It did not get up.

"I guess you know me this time," Yoshi said. She walked straight ahead to school. Mr. Pine smiled when he saw her. "You remembered your promise. You're on time!"

Yoshi looked straight at Mr. Pine. She said, "Roady Roadrunner helped me."

Aquí Está Mi Nieta[1]

Ana Rosa had come to stay with her grandmother in Texas and go to Mesa Adventist School there. On the first morning Grandmother walked to school with Ana Rosa. They were speaking in Spanish. At Mesa Adventist School Ana Rosa would speak English and learn some new words.

"You will find new friends here, Ana Rosa," her grandmother said. "They will help you with the new English words."

Ana Rosa nodded. She was looking at the tall flagpole in front of the school. Two boys were raising the flag.

Her grandmother called to one of them, "Eduardo, aquí está mi nieta !"

[1] Aquí Está Mi Nieta (ah·KEE e·STAH MEE NEAY·tah)

Eduardo ran to meet them. He spoke to Ana Rosa in English. "Hi! Let's go to our room. Everyone wants to see you!"

To her grandmother he said, "I'll show her the way home after school." And he led Ana Rosa to the classroom.

The teacher said, "Welcome, Ana Rosa." "Why don't you sit at Eduardo's table?" she suggested. "Then he can help you."

"Thank you," said Ana Rosa.

Everyone was smiling at her. These new friends were giving her a good welcome.

"Oh," she thought as she listened to the new sounds, "it's easy to understand."

Just before closing time the teacher said, "Let's go out to the playground to show Ana Rosa what we know about our shadows."

"Let's show her where her shadow is when the afternoon sun is behind her in the west," someone suggested.

"I'll trace her shadow on a long sheet of paper," Eduardo said.

Ana Rosa did not know the English word "shadow," so she did not understand the talk. And why was everyone going outdoors?

65

At a sunny spot on the sidewalk Eduardo said, "Turn your back to the sun, Ana Rosa." He pointed in the right direction.

He unrolled the paper on the walk in front of her feet. With a big black marker he traced the outline of her shadow. It was almost as long as the sheet of paper.

The children pointed in the direction of the sun. "There's the sun behind you in the west. Your shadow's in front of you. What does that tell you, Ana Rosa?" they asked.

Ana Rosa did not understand. The teacher tried to help her. "The sun is in the west in the afternoon, Ana Rosa. Your shadow helps to show you where the west is."

But no one helped Ana Rosa with the new English word "shadow." It was like being lost and not finding the way.

Eduardo understood. "Never mind," he suggested softly to her in Spanish. "On our way home your shadow will be in front of you. That's all you need to remember."

The school bell rang, and it was time to go home.

"Meet me at the flagpole," Eduardo said.

Ana Rosa said good-by to her new friends and walked to the flagpole.

The flag was gone, and so was Eduardo. Where was he? How could she find her way home? She waited on the walk. She looked in all directions. Everything looked strange. "Help me, Jesus," she prayed.

She looked down at the sidewalk. Her own black shadow was in front of her feet. It was like finding a friend.

"My shadow," Ana Rosa said in Spanish. She said it again in English. And this time she remembered Eduardo's words.

Could the shadow lead her in the right direction? Could it lead Ana Rosa back to her grandmother's house?

Ana Rosa took a step forward. The shadow moved forward too. The sun was behind her. She walked on, finding a way while her shadow stayed in front of her. She let the shadow lead her until she heard Eduardo's voice behind her, calling, "Ana Rosa, wait for me!"

When he reached her, he pointed to a house just ahead of them. "There's your grandmother's house," he said. "You knew how to find your way alone, didn't you?"

"With my shadow to show me," Ana Rosa said, "it was easy!"

69

The Mystery of the Suitcase

Mrs. Emory lived in a little house. Her kitchen door looked out on tall trees. In the summer the kitchen door stood wide open.

Charles Workman lived in a big two-story house nearby. The Workman family were new in the neighborhood. Charles and Mrs. Emory had become good friends. He liked to sit on the steps outside her door and watch her make cookies.

Day after day Mrs. Emory made cookies in her kitchen. No one in the neighborhood knew why. Those cookies were a mystery. But Charles did know what kind of cookies they were.

On Monday Mrs. Emory always made raisin cookies. Monday was a spicy day.

On Tuesday she baked brownies. The air around the kitchen was pretty sweet on Tuesday.

The next day she made peanut-butter cookies. Charles Workman liked these best.

Thursday cookies were never the same.

"Thursday is my leftover day," Mrs. Emory said.

And the last cooky day of each week was for Mrs. Emory's special, own crunchy oatmeal cookies.

On Sunday morning Mrs. Emory went off on a six o'clock bus. Where she went was a mystery. She took a heavy, old suitcase. She came home in the evening on a six o'clock bus. Then the suitcase was heavier.

Charles liked to carry the suitcase to the bus and carry it home again at night. Mrs. Emory always said, "Are you strong enough to carry the suitcase today? It's heavy."

He knew he was strong enough! At the bus he watched Mrs. Emory hop aboard. She was as quick as anything. Her hair was white. Her shoes were old and a little too big. Her coat was long, and so were her skirts. Her hat was green.

Charles handed the heavy suitcase up to her, and she handed him a bag. "Here is your pay, and thank you, Charles Workman. I don't aim to be beholden."

The pay was exactly the same every week— three Monday cookies, two Tuesday cookies, and one each for the other three days.

One Sunday night he waited and waited. "Mom," he called when he came home. "Mrs. Emory is never this late. I wonder where she is."

His mother said, "She's a mystery to me."

Charles shook his head, "I think Mrs. Emory takes those cookies somewhere special."

"Maybe she sells them," suggested his mother. "Are her cookies good enough to sell, Charles?"

"They sure are! I like them a lot and I like Mrs. Emory too. She is one of my best friends. But I do wonder what is making her so late today."

On Monday morning Charles went over to the kitchen door and peeked in Mrs. Emory's window. The house seemed too still.

"I wonder where she can be?" he asked himself again. "There's no one here."

But behind him, he heard someone say, "Looking for something?" A police officer was looking at him.

"I am looking for Mrs. Emory," Charles
answered. "She never says where she is
going, but she always comes home at night.
Her suitcase is very heavy then, and I help
her carry it. Last night she never came."

The police officer made some notes in a
book. Charles's father came hurrying across
the garden. "What is going on here?" Mr.
Workman asked.

The officer answered, "Your son is worried about your neighbor. Quite a detective you have in your family, sir."

"Mrs. Emory? She comes and goes with her old, heavy suitcase. That's all we know about her. She is a neighborhood mystery."

"Oh, Dad," Charles cried. "She's my friend, and I do wonder where she is now!"

The officer smiled. "She is spending a few days in the City Hospital. She is having a little rest in her other home."

How could a hospital be her home?

The officer was saying, "Mrs. Emory worked in the hospital kitchen for a long time, making special cookies for children. They liked her cookies best of all."

"So she takes her cookies to children in the hospital. But why is that suitcase so heavy when she comes home?" Charles asked.

"That suitcase is full of special things for making more cookies. The hospital gives them to her," the officer answered.

"Do they pay her for making the cookies?"

"No, indeed. She likes to do it for the children," the officer said. "When she needs a rest, she uses a hospital room. She'll be home soon, as lively as ever."

Charles said slowly, "She's going to need me. I'll be waiting for her so I can carry that suitcase. Please tell her I'll be ready."

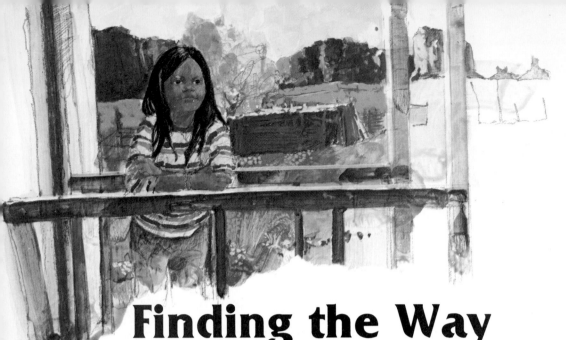

Finding the Way

Sharon stood in the doorway of her grandfather's house. She looked across the valley. How different it was from the city.

Here on the reservation the only sounds were from the birds and the wind. The nearest house was two miles away. It was land her family had lived on for many, many years.

Right now Grandfather was working in his fine garden. Sharon's mother had gone to visit an old friend. She would be away all morning. What is there for me to do, Sharon wondered.

Then she noticed the little burro standing in the field. "May I take Maria a carrot?" she asked her grandfather.

"Nothing to stop you," he said.

Sharon took the carrot and went down the path to the field. The burro looked up. She pointed her long ears to Sharon. Sharon fed her the carrot. She stroked the soft fur of the burro's ears. Maria finished the carrot and nudged Sharon.

"So you want to go," laughed Sharon. Maria was tied to a stake in the ground. Sharon untied the rope. Then, standing on a rock, she climbed onto the burro's back.

"Maria and I are going to hunt for some acorns. I will be back soon," she called to her grandfather.

They headed up the mountain. Soon Sharon saw acorns on the ground. She knew her ancestors made bread from acorns in the old days. She slid off Maria's back. She filled her pockets with acorns.

After a while they came out into an open meadow. They went very slowly. Maria kept finding things to eat. Finally, Sharon stopped. She sat down on a big rock.

In the rock were some small holes. "That's where Indians used to grind their acorns," she told Maria.

She put some acorns in one hole. Then she hunted for a rock to pound them with. Pounding took two hands. She let go of the rope. "Don't wander away," she told Maria.

Grinding the acorns was hard work. Her arms grew tired. And oh, how hot she was! She stopped to rest and looked around for Maria. The burro was nowhere to be seen. "Maria!" she called. "Maria!"

Sharon climbed to the top of the big rock. She looked and listened. There was no sign of the burro. But strange sounds seemed to be all around her.

"Maria left me alone," she whispered. Then she thought of Grandfather. "Be coolheaded and trust God," he always said.

She saw something moving on the far side of the clearing. Could it be a wildcat? What made the leaves rustle so? Was it a snake? Everything looked and sounded strange and scary. She wanted to be home, even without Maria. She wasn't sure where home was. But she had to get there. Fear grabbed her.

She turned and ran. The ground was very rough. Soon she knew that this was not the way they had come.

Suddenly she stepped on a loose stone and fell down. Her knee stung. She felt like crying. She wanted to stay on the ground. But she knew she must get home. She also knew she was lost. What should she do?

Grandfather's words came to her mind. "I forgot my best help," thought Sharon. "I forgot to be coolheaded and trust God." Then she asked God to help her get home.

As she sat up, she heard the sound of hoofs. There came the burro!

Maria nudged Sharon. Sharon climbed on Maria's back. "Oh, Maria, I thought I'd lost you. And here you've found me."

Maria started off, but not the way Sharon had been going. She went the other way. Sharon said nothing. "I will trust," she thought. And her fears left her.

Around the side of a hill and through some trees they went. Suddenly they came out into the open. There, next to a field of corn, was Grandfather's house.

Maria moved faster. Sharon forgot all about her knee. She yelled. There, standing on the porch, were her mother and grandfather. How wonderful it was to be home!

"What have you been doing?" her mother asked when she saw Sharon's knee.

"I've been making acorn bread like my ancestors," Sharon answered. Then looking down at her knee, she added, "And I learned to be coolheaded and trust."

Her grandfather's eyes twinkled, but he asked no questions.

Take the Right Road

Help the roadrunner find the rattlesnake. Follow only the road that has on it words with the same vowel sounds as in *bite* and *head*. Watch the forks in the road. If you take a wrong turn, go back and try another road.

Begin with the roadrunner and the word *bite.* You must end at the snake and the word *head.*

Think of a New Ending

Speck

Tell how Speck might have acted at the end of the story if Ben hadn't trained him to "fetch."

Roady Roadrunner and Yoshi

How might the story have been different if Yoshi had not fed the roadrunner and made a pet of it?

Aquí Está Mi Nieta

If Ana Rosa had not learned about the sun and her shadow, how might the story have ended?

The Mystery of the Suitcase

How would the story change if no one knew where Mrs. Emory was?

Finding the Way

What might have happened to Sharon if the burro had not known the way back home?

Opening New Doors

Sam and His Cart

Whr-r-r, whr-r-r, round and round went the big back wheels of Sam's cart. The spokes shone like silver and the wheels flashed.

Sam needed his cart because he could not walk like other kids. Sam was born handicapped.

Sam could not talk as well as other kids. Sam could not hold still, so he just shook, and shook, and shook. But Sam could think and Sam could work. And Sam had a cart that opened doors for him.

When Sam was twelve, Sam began to work. Sam sold lightbulbs from door to door, from house to house, to make money.

But Sam, who liked kids, made some kids scared. They didn't understand why he shook, and why he couldn't talk, and why he had a cart. His world was not like their world.

But most kids were friendly, and they asked lots and lots of questions: "Why do you ride in a cart?" "Why do you shake so much?" "Why can't you talk like us?"

Sam liked to talk to people so he tried to answer questions. It made him feel good, and sometimes he made friends.

But sometimes grown-ups were scared too. Sometimes they would tell their kids to stay away from Sam.

One day the sun was shining. It was a good day to sell. Sam rode in his cart down the street from door to door, from house to house, selling lightbulbs.

Sam stopped at a great big white house. Five kids made a circle around Sam and asked him, "Why do you shake?" "Why can't you talk right?"

Sam said, "I was born this way and I can't stop shaking. I can't talk right either, but I have a cart. Do you have a cart?"

Just then a young woman came to the door. "Children, you stay away from that boy. You don't know him. You might hurt him. You know that your dad doesn't like you to talk to strangers." The kids ran off and the young woman closed the door.

Sam went back to work. He rode up the driveway and rang the doorbell at the side door. The same young woman came to the door and shouted, "What do you want?"

"Do you want to buy some lightbulbs?"

The lady shouted, "No, I don't. Go away."

Sam was tired and unhappy and he began to cry. He tried to talk to the young woman, but she could not understand. So the young woman went next door and brought a neighbor lady back with her. The neighbor lady was old and wore a black dress and walked with a crooked cane.

The neighbor lady gave Sam a cookie and a glass of water. The cookie crunched comfortably between his teeth. The water cooled his throat.

The young woman said that Sam should not be allowed to go out on the street. He might get hit by a car or something. The lady with the crooked cane said to the young woman, "A car might hit me too."

The young woman said, "Well, that's different." Just then a red car drove up the driveway. A man got out and wanted to know what was wrong. The man was the young woman's husband.

He drove Sam and his cart home. The man told Sam's daddy, "This boy should not be on the streets. He might get hurt."

II

For a long, long time, Sam stayed home. He stayed home and played with his dog. He stayed home and felt lonely. He stayed home and didn't work. He shut himself up in his own little world.

Sam asked his daddy, "Why do I scare people? Why can't I talk like most people? Why do I shake all the time?"

Sam's daddy said, "You scare people because you are different. You are handicapped. You can't talk like most people and you shake all the time because you have cerebral palsy. You were born that way. Cerebral palsy makes your brain give the wrong directions to your muscles."

Sam said, "Oh, I see," but he really didn't see. He could only see that he spilled his milk every time he tried to drink it.

Then one day, knock, knock on the door, and the lady with the crooked cane was standing there with a box of cookies. "May I come in and talk to you?" she said.

Sam said, "Sure."

The lady with the crooked cane went into the house and asked Sam why he didn't sell lightbulbs anymore.

"Because I scare people. They think I will hurt them and that I might get hurt," said Sam.

The lady with a crooked cane said, "I've been talking to some people in the neighborhood. We have missed you. Some of us want to buy lightbulbs. When will you come around to our houses to take orders?"

So the next day, Sam went around to the neighborhood of the lady with the crooked cane. He sold lots and lots of lightbulbs.

And once again Sam sold lightbulbs door to door, house to house.

Some kids were still scared of Sam, and some grown-ups still told their kids not to go near Sam and not to bother him.

But some people told Sam how proud they were of him and some people gave him extra money.

Every day that the sun shone, Sam would go out in his cart and sell lightbulbs door to door.

Sam would ride down the street in his cart and shake, and shake, and shake. Sam could not talk like the other kids, but he could think and he could work.

Whr-r-r, whr-r-r, round and round went the big back wheels of Sam's cart. The spokes shone like silver and the wheels flashed when they rolled.

Sam grew up and wrote stories. This is one of them.

I Like Old Clothes

I like old clothes,
Hand-me-down clothes,
Worn outgrown clothes,
Not-my-own clothes.
When somebody grows
And gives me her clothes,
I don't say, "What, *those?*"
And turn up my nose
The way some people do
When their clothes aren't new.

I *like* old clothes.
I really do.
Clothes with a history,
Clothes with a mystery,
Sweaters and shirts
That are brother-and-sistery,

Clothes that belonged
   to a friend of a friend
Who wore them to school
   when she lived in East Bend.
"You lived in East Bend once,
   Blue Sweater," I say.
"Just think, you are living
   in my town today."

I like old clothes,
Faded-out clothes,
Not-so-new clothes,
Where-were-you clothes;
And each time I wear them
I try to imagine
The places they've seen
And whose clothes they'll be
When they're finished with me.
—*Mary Ann Hoberman*

Mr. Blynn's Crazy Kite

Andy and his friends were playing ball on the Campbells' farm. It was almost too windy to play ball. The sun was already setting. It was bright, bright red.

Andy was catching a ball. Up it sailed high into the air, and down it came into his mitt.

"Wow!" Andy Campbell and Ed Miller shouted.

Mrs. Campbell was watching from the back porch of the house. "You have far-seeing eyes, Andy," she said.

It was true. Andy's far-seeing eyes could find beetles touring around a meadow. He could see small birds hiding in the leaves of a tree. And when Mr. Blynn's kites sailed high in the air, Andy could track them touring across the sky.

Mr. Blynn was a farmer. When he finished his farm work, he made kites in a small workshop in an open meadow.

Some of the kites were five feet long. They had strange shapes. One was a big flat owl. One was curved at both ends.

Andy's favorite kite looked like a huge arrowhead. One end was pointed. The other end looked like a pair of wings.

It was fun watching Mr. Blynn fly his kites. Sometimes they dipped and crashed. Sometimes they flew out of sight. A few of them broke loose. Andy's far-seeing eyes helped Mr. Blynn track them across the sky.

Those far-seeing eyes helped Andy to catch balls pretty well too.

Mrs. Campbell called, "Do your best now, Andy. Time for one more throw. It's already suppertime." Then she went into the house.

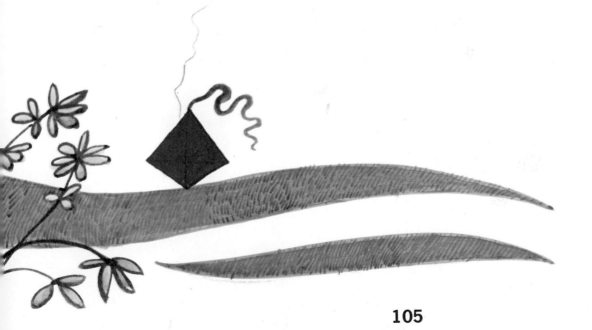

"Throw the ball as high as you can," Bobby Brown yelled. "We'll try to catch it."

The ball soared into the air. Andy watched it go. Suddenly a strange object appeared in the sky. It glowed with reddish light.

What a queer thing it was! It looked like a saucer with a cup upside down on it.

Andy forgot about catching the ball. He stared and stared at the strange object. The other children were staring at it too.

Bobby said, "Say, is that thing a flying saucer?" She ran across fields trying to keep up with the strange moving object.

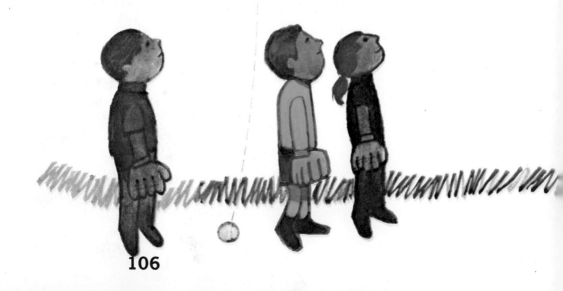

Mrs. Campbell called, "What's going on?"

Ed Miller jumped up and down. He pointed at the object. "Call the police, Mrs. Campbell. There's a flying saucer!"

Andy's far-seeing eyes were already tracking the reddish glow. "Mr. Blynn will want to see this," he decided.

So Andy hopped on his bike and headed for Mr. Blynn's meadow.

Mr. Blynn was standing in the meadow and staring up at the strange object. In one hand he held some loose twine, and he was laughing to himself.

"Well, Andy," Mr. Blynn said. "What do you think that is up there?"

"Is it a flying saucer?" Andy wondered. "With a cabin on top? It looks like one, all reddish and moving so fast."

"Wind's moving fast too," Mr. Blynn answered. "Did you notice that?"

"I forgot about the wind," Andy said.

"There's enough wind to give a kite a good lift of air," Mr. Blynn said. "A good lift of air is what makes it fun to fly a kite. I like to see what happens then."

Andy said slowly, "But that thing doesn't look like a kite, does it? What's that reddish light in the top part of it?"

The strange object was moving farther and farther away from them.

"Take one last look," Mr. Blynn suggested.

Andy squinted. "Maybe that is your kite, sir. I can see the pointed end and the wings. But what about that thing on top?"

Mr. Blynn smiled. "Maybe my kite and a weather balloon got mixed up with each other. Maybe they tangled. I guess a small instrument on the balloon tangled with my kite string and the kite broke loose."

Mr. Blynn let the loose string hang from his hand. He said, "Yes, sir, the kite broke loose, and the wind is carrying those two along together. That's my guess."

Andy had another question. "But how about that reddish light?"

Mr. Blynn winked. "Did you notice how red the sun was when it was setting?"

"Yes, sir. I noticed it when I was catching a ball over at the Campbells' farm."

"Well," Mr. Blynn said, "I guess the balloon-kite was up high too. High enough to catch some of the sun's reddish light."

Mr. Blynn looked at Andy and winked again. "That's your flying saucer, Andy."

They both laughed.

"Yes, sir, Mr. Blynn, I guess it is. I'll go and tell my friends." And off went Andy to tell the news.

FLYING KITE

I OFTEN sit and wish that I
Could be a kite up in the sky,
And ride upon the breeze, and go
Whatever way it chanced to blow.
Then I could look beyond the town,
And see the river winding down,
And follow all the ships that sail
Like me before the merry gale,
Until at last with them I came
To some place with a foreign name.

Frank Dempster Sherman

SPECIAL VISITORS

One summer Jeff and his family worked at an Adventist youth camp high in the Rocky Mountains. It was near big woods, where hummingbirds live in the trees.

"They are so tiny and they fly so fast," Jeff said to his father. "How can I ever see what they look like?"

"We can set up a feeder for the hummingbirds," his father said. "We will set it up here at the cabin. Then some tiny hummers will surely come."

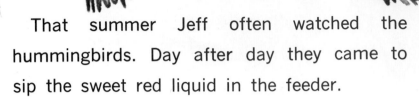

That summer Jeff often watched the hummingbirds. Day after day they came to sip the sweet red liquid in the feeder.

One day a beautiful male broad-tail came to the feeder. It sipped the sweet red liquid and was gone with a flash of its whirring wings. Then something like a tiny green helicopter moved through the air. A plain buffy-breasted hummer was coming to taste the red food. The flashy male whirred down and chased the buffy-breasted hummer into the woods. Back he came with a noisy whirr and perched on a limb of the tree.

Over and over that bossy male broad-tail chased away the other birds. Finally one hummingbird led the male far away through the trees. Other hummingbirds came and fed, until the bossy male chased them off.

"Where do they go in the woods?" Jeff wondered. "I wish I could find their nests."

Jeff had seen pictures of hummingbirds' nests in books. But he did want to see a real nest. He knew they were very small. He knew they were hard to find in the woods.

Day after day Jeff tracked a special path through the woods. He followed the birds when they left the feeder. He followed their flashing colors among the trees. He listened for their whirring wings. But summer was going fast, and he was still looking for a hummingbird's nest.

One chilly morning Jeff left the cabin after breakfast. He had on his red shirt. Hummingbirds like the color red. They often come near it, as they did to the feeder.

Jeff walked along his special path. He heard the hummers. Whirring wings came near. A tiny hummingbird was coming toward Jeff's red shirt. The bird dipped once. The whirring sound stopped. Jeff felt a very soft touch on his arm.

Then the buffy-breasted green hummer flew off to feed on some red flowers.

Jeff waited. When the tiny bird flew off into the woods, he tried to follow. He pushed through low branches of the trees. The nest must be near! But he could not find it.

He turned to leave the woods, and there was the nest close enough to touch. It was only as big as a nut shell. It looked like the other knots on the tree branch. But this knot was a nest. A hummingbird was in it.

Jeff walked around the nest. The small buffy-breasted mother's eyes followed him. She made little frightened fluttery sounds. Jeff stepped still closer. Away she flew. He tiptoed up and peeked down into the nest. He saw two very tiny eggs. They looked like small white beans.

Jeff reached out to touch them. He stopped, jamming his hands into his pockets. "No!" he said to himself, "I won't touch them."

He turned away from the nest. Very, very slowly, Jeff walked home.

117

He was late for lunch. His mother asked, "Where have you been all morning, Jeff?"

"Oh, in the woods. Dad, how long does it take for a baby hummingbird to fly?"

"Quite a while, Jeff."

"Can babies eat out of our feeder?"

"Yes, if they have a wire to perch on."

"Dad, will you help me put a wire perch on our feeder?"

"Sure, Jeff." With a smile his father asked, "Are you waiting for special visitors?"

"I just want to be ready," Jeff answered.

He helped his father bend a wire around the feeding tube. He kept the feeder filled. Hummingbirds came and went from the feeder. For quite a while every day, Jeff watched them sip the sweet colored liquid.

"How about those special visitors?" his Dad asked. "It's about time for them to come, isn't it?"

"Maybe," Jeff said. It was hard to wait and to keep on watching. But he did do it.

One morning a mother hummer and two baby hummers did come to the feeder. Jeff watched the babies with their short bills. One at a time the tiny hummers perched on the wire. They sipped the sweet red liquid.

Then they followed the mother bird into the woods. Jeff watched them go.

"Am I glad you hatched!" he called.

TREES

Trees are the kindest things I know,
They do no harm, they simply grow

And spread a shade for sleepy cows,
And gather birds among their boughs.

They give us fruit in leaves above
And wood to make our houses of,

And leaves to burn on Hallowe'en,
And in the Spring new buds of green.

They are the first when day's begun
To touch the beams of morning sun,

They are the last to hold the light
When evening changes into night,

And when a moon floats on the sky
They hum a drowsy lullaby,

Of sleepy children long ago . . .
Trees are the kindest things I know.

     —*Harry Behn*

Talking without Words

Sam could not talk as well as others. People had a hard time knowing what he said. Some people who cannot talk use signs. Think of Sam and other people who can't talk when you do the exercise below.

1. What is the difference between making sounds and talking?
   Do you ever make sounds with your mouth without words? When and how?

2. Show you are surprised without using words. Now show these feelings without using words.
afraid	cold	happy	hot
angry	sleepy	hurt	sad

3. Suppose a new boy or girl in your classroom cannot speak English. How would you talk to him or her? How would he or she answer?
   Try these questions. How would you answer these questions without using words?
   How old are you?
   What is your name?
   Have you a dog?
   What game do you like to play?

4. Blindfold a friend and hand him or her an object. Let the friend feel the shape, size, and weight and guess what the object is. Use such objects as a pencil, orange, feather, eraser, and twig. Find other objects and play the game with another friend.

A Kite Puzzle

Read the first clue to the puzzle and find the answer in the lists below. Count the number of blanks for the first clue on the kite and be sure that your answer has the same number of letters. Do the rest in the same way. Write your answers on a piece of paper.

1. A place to fly a kite
2. People and animals drink this
3. What you hold to fly a kite
4. Something that flies straight up and down
5. To feel with the fingers
6. Words in order
7. It means only one
8. Where kites fly

liquid	meadow	visitors
object	single	reddish
field	sky	buffy-breasted
string	twine	sentences
touch		hummingbird

Animals Are Fun Too

The Rescue

The terrible storm was finally over.

Ramón[1] Perez leaned the hayfork against the wall and listened. Was that a groan that seemed to come from the hay shed?

Ramón ran outside. Papá[2] was sitting with closed eyes leaning against the shed. He was moaning softly. The heavy rain had caused an old post to give way, letting a part of the roof fall. It must have hit Papá.

"I'll go get Mamá,"[3] said Ramón.

Papá opened his eyes. "I can walk if you help me,". he said. As they struggled toward the house Papá asked, "Did you shut the geese in the shed?"

"Yes, Papá," said Ramón.

---

[1] (ray-MOHN); [2] (pə-PAH); [3] (mə-MAH)

Those geese! There were dozens of the big white geese. They were turned into the strawberry fields in the spring to eat the weeds.

Mamá knew something was wrong when she saw Ramón and Papá coming. She held the sagging screen door open. "Call the doctor," Mamá said to Ramón as she helped Papá to the bedroom.

Ramón picked up the telephone. "The phone doesn't work, Mamá," he said. "I will run to the neighbors."

Mamá followed Ramón out the door. "Hurry!" she said. "Papá is hurt on the inside."

Ramón started to run. His bare feet squished in the muddy places. The neighbor's house was a long way down the road. Ramón saw the damage the storm had done. Fences were down. The creek was swirling with muddy water.

When Ramón got to the place where he was to cross the bridge, he got the greatest shock. The bridge was gone! There was no way for him to get to the house down the road. "I must get help fast," Ramón thought. "But how?"

It would be dark soon. He shook his head and turned to go back home.

As he neared the house Ramón heard a roar. A helicopter! Someone must be checking the storm damage. Quickly Ramón pulled off his yellow shirt and waved it over his head. Would they see it? For a minute the helicopter seemed to stand still. Then it flew toward the mountain. It might come back soon. If only there were some way. . . .

The geese in the shed were "talking" softly among themselves. Probably they were waiting for food. They were always hungry.

Suddenly Ramón's eyes lit up. He ran to the grain shed. If only he had time. . . .

Before darkness had settled on the land, Ramón heard the roar of the returning helicopter. For an awful minute it flew toward town. Then it turned and came back and settled down by the back gate.

Soon Papá was on his way to the doctor.

Before long the helicopter was back. The pilot told Mamá and Ramón that Papá had a broken rib. He would be home in a few days.

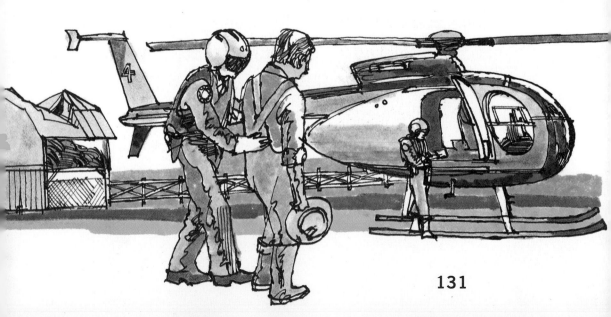

The pilot looked at Ramón. "How did you think of it?" he asked. "I was never more surprised in my life."

"It came to me when you flew over the first time and I heard the geese. They are always ready to eat. I knew if I put corn on the ground they would come running when I opened the door."

The pilot grinned. "And I looked down and saw a big S-O-S of white geese on the wet black ground."

Ramón smiled. "I saved enough corn to mark a trail back to the shed after you left. And then I gave them a bit more. I thought they had earned it."

Bears Aren't Everywhere[1]

One night Danny's mother read him a book about bears. The book was about brown bears and black bears, cinnamon bears and a polar bear.

Then Danny's mother put out the light and said, "Good night, sleep tight, Danny."

But Danny did not sleep tight.

Danny lay in bed and thought about bears.

All of a sudden bears seemed to be everywhere—brown bears, black bears, cinnamon bears. And a polar bear was at the window.

The next morning Danny forgot all about the bears. He helped his father feed the chickens and bring in the eggs from the nests. Then Danny went exploring.

He climbed the hill behind the farmhouse. He stood high on the hill and looked down on the farm below. The cold wind blew in his face.

Danny saw that everything was changing. The goldenrod had changed from gold to golden brown. The leaves on some of the trees were changing from green to orange, red, and yellow.

Then Danny ran down the hill to the orchard. He saw that the apples were changing too. They were turning from sour green to red and yellow.

Danny did some exploring. He looked into the hole where a woodchuck lived. But the woodchuck wasn't at home.

"I think the woodchuck must be out eating someplace," said Danny to himself. "It wants to get as fat as it can, so that it can have a good sleep in the winter."

Danny climbed over the old stone wall, but just as he got to the edge of the woods, he heard a noise.

What kind of a noise was that—or was it a noise at all?

It wasn't a bong or a bang.

It was more of a crackle or crunch.

Danny thought about the bears in his dream—brown bears, black bears, cinnamon bears, and the polar bear he had seen at his window.

He walked as quietly as he could walk, over the old stone wall, through the orchard.

Then he ran. Danny ran as fast as he could run.

"There's a bear down there," yelled Danny to his mother, as he slammed the kitchen door.

When Danny's father came in from milking the cows that night, Danny said, "There's a bear down there."

"Where, down there?" asked Danny's father.

"Down below the orchard in the woods," Danny answered.

"Then you and I will go down to the woods in the morning and find the bear," Danny's father said.

But Danny didn't want to go down to the woods with his father. He didn't want to go exploring and find the bear.

When Danny went to bed that night, the bears were everywhere—brown bears, black bears, cinnamon bears, and the polar bear at the window.

"What kind of a bear is waiting in the woods down there?" said Danny to himself.

Then he put his head under the covers, and the bears all went away.

When Danny woke up in the morning, he couldn't see a thing. The fields, the trees, the barn—all the world around his house was covered with a soft white fog.

No wind was blowing. Everything was still.

"Come on, Danny," Danny's father said after breakfast. "We're going down to find the bear."

"Not this morning," Danny said. "I have to feed the chickens and bring in the eggs."

"Oh, no," Danny's father said. "I need you, Danny. I need you to show me where the bear is hiding in the woods."

So Danny had to go with his father to the woods to find the bear.

Danny and his father walked down the hill together. They walked in the still white fog.

His father said, "Put your feet down carefully. Don't make any noise."

When they came to the orchard, Danny and his father stood still and listened.

And sure enough!

Danny heard the noise again.

It wasn't a bong or a bang.

It was more of a crackle and crunch.

"There's the bear," Danny said very softly.

A soft wind blew.

The white fog swirled around.

Danny and his father stood very still and listened.

Danny didn't want to go exploring over the old stone wall and into the woods. Danny just wanted to run home as fast as he could run. He wanted to slam the kitchen door.

But Danny's father took his hand, and they went over the wall and into the woods together.

There was the noise again.

Not a bong or a bang, but a crackle and crunch, in the dry leaves scattered on the ground.

Danny stopped and looked and listened.

Just then a fat gray squirrel ran up the trunk of a great big walnut tree. When the squirrel leaped from branch to branch to branch, it shook walnuts down. They fell with a crunch and crackle into the dry leaves scattered on the ground.

Danny laughed and so did his father.

"Some bear," Danny said.

His father smiled. "I guess bears aren't really everywhere, are they, Danny?"

"I guess not," Danny said.

"And don't you think," said Danny's father, "that it would be better to be SURE it's a bear, before you get so frightened of a bear that's not even there?"

Danny knew that his father was right.

"My bear was just a fat gray squirrel getting ready for winter," Danny said.

"That's a good idea," said his father.

So Danny and his father filled their pockets full of walnuts and took them home to dry.

A long time after that Danny sat beside the fire and cracked his walnuts, while the wind blew against the window and the snow was deep outside.

"I wonder," Danny said, "if underneath the snow someplace, or in some hollow tree—"

"A big brown bear is waiting for you?" Danny's father said.

"No," laughed Danny, "but I wonder if underneath the snow someplace, or in some hollow tree, that fat gray squirrel is eating walnuts just like me?"

Kookaburra

Mother stood in the backyard and called, "Lance! Lance! Time to come in and study." She waited. She heard many sounds but she didn't hear Lance.

Lance lived in Australia, far out in the bush with his mother and father. No neighbors lived nearby. No school was near. His mother taught him at home.

Mother called again, "Lance! Lance!"

"I'm right here," Lance said as he came out from behind a gum tree.

"Have you been hiding?" Mother asked.

"No," Lance said. "I was in the bush listening to the bird sounds. I didn't hear you until just now."

Mother smiled. "Well, it's time to study. Let's study birds today. Maybe you can learn something new about the kookaburras."

Mother and Lance went inside. They got the bird book and Lance began to read:

"Kookaburra is the name of a bird from Australia. The word *kookaburra* was made up by the first people of Australia.

"The kookaburra makes seven kinds of sounds. One is a laughing song that sounds like 'ooo, ooo, ooo, ha, ha, ha.'

"Another call sounds like 'Kooaa, kooaa.' This sound may be why Australia's first people named it the Kookaburra."

There was a picture of the kookaburra. It looked like this:

KOOKABURRA

"I didn't know the kookaburra made seven different sounds," Lance said. "I'd like to go and listen to the sounds again."

"A good idea," said his mother. "Maybe you can watch a kookaburra and see how it lives. But let's do a little more schoolwork first."

After he and Mother had done some math, Lance went to the bush to listen to the kookaburras.

Lance knew the bush well. It was his playground. His father had hung a rope from a tree to make a swing. He even had a tree house made of branches and leaves.

Lance sat down in the swing and listened. He heard the wind sliding through the trees. He heard the rushing of leaves as a field mouse ran by. He listened for bird sounds. He listened very hard for the kookaburra call.

First, he heard the "caw, caw, caw" of the crow. Then he heard the "qua, qua, qua" of the magpies. Then, very softly, there it was: "ooo, ooo, ooo."

Lance stopped the swing and stood up. He looked around. Then he heard it again: "ooo, ooo, ooo" followed by the laughing sound "ha, ha, ha."

He turned around slowly and there it was! A kookaburra!

The kookaburra was sitting on the branch of a tree. Lance quietly tiptoed toward another tree with a low branch. The kookaburra went on singing "ha, ha, ha!" Lance slowly started to climb the other tree.

Quick as a flash the kookaburra called, "kooaa, kooaa, kooaa," and dived. Lance ducked. The kookaburra flew to a tree hole above Lance's head. He was very upset.

"So that's it," thought Lance as he climbed down. "There's a nest in the tree, and the kookaburra wants to keep me away."

Lance went back to his swing and waited. He waited and watched.

After a while, the kookaburra flew away from the tree hole.

Lance ran over to the tree and quickly climbed up on the branch again. This time he held on to the tree and stood up on the branch. He could see inside the hole. It had no leaves. It had no sticks. It had nothing except three small white eggs.

Lance was so happy he almost forgot where the kookaburra was.

Then he heard, "kooaa, kooaa, kooaa." The kookaburra was back. Lance ducked just in time and jumped down out of the tree.

He ran home and told his mother about the kookaburra and the eggs.

"When will they hatch?" he asked her.

She looked in the bird book and said, "In about three or four weeks."

"So long?" asked Lance. His mother laughed.

"Well, the chicks have to have time to grow inside the egg," she said.

"I guess so," said Lance.

"Here," said his mother as she showed him the book. "This is what they will look like when they hatch."

Every day Lance went to the bush. From his tree house he could see the tree hole. But the kookaburras couldn't see him.

Now there were three kookaburras. They took turns going in the hole to warm the eggs.

First one would go in and stay for a while. Then one of the kookaburras on the tree branch would call, "kooaa." The "kooaa," which was very soft, would be followed by a "chu-chu-chu" sound.

The bird inside would then come to the front of the hole. It would answer, "kooaa, chu-chu-chu." Then they would take each other's place.

Every day for almost three weeks Lance watched as the kookaburras flew in and out of the tree hole nest.

One day Lance saw that one of the kookaburras had a worm in its mouth. And it was taking the worm into the tree hole!

Lance looked at the other kookaburra. It wasn't just sitting and waiting. One at a time, the kookaburras flew away. When they came back, each had something in its mouth.

"They've hatched, they've hatched!" said Lance. "The chicks have hatched at last!"

Lance ran home and told his mother and father.

"Now I can bring one home," he said.

"What do you mean by that, Lance?" asked his mother.

"You know, Mother. I can bring home one of the chicks and have it for a pet," he said.

"Oh, no, Lance," said his mother.

"That wouldn't be a good idea, son," said his father.

"Why not?" asked Lance. "I would find worms for it to eat. I would feed it and take it everywhere with me," he said.

"But kookaburras belong in the wild. They need to be free," said his father.

Lance began to cry.

"Don't cry, Lance," said his mother. She put her arms around him and held him.

"Now, now, son," said his father. "Remember that song we used to sing?" He began to sing:

"Kookaburra sits on the old gum tree.
Merry merry king of the bush is he.
Laugh, kookaburra. Laugh kookaburra.
Free your life must be."

Soon Lance started to sing too.

They sang in a round. First Father would sing the first line. As soon as he got to the second line, Lance would begin to sing the first line. When Lance got to the second line, Mother would come in with the first line.

They sang it over and over again. Then Lance said to Mother and Father, "Let's go for a walk now."

So they followed Lance into the bush. He showed them the tree and the nest.

They watched the kookaburras flying.

"I won't have a pet kookaburra," said Lance. "The kookaburras will stay in the bush and be my friends. One day, the chicks will fly. They will fly and they will be free."

"Kooaa, kooaa, kooaa," called the kookaburras. "Ooo, ooo, ooo. Ha, ha, ha," they laughed.

THE INVITATION

Nancy Ann walked down the country road. She was on her way home from school. In her hand was a picture of the schoolhouse, cut out of red paper. On it was written: "Come to the fair! At Lone Oak Adventist School, Sunday at 2 o'clock."

Michael caught up with her. He and Nancy Ann were both in the same grade. They lived near each other, and they often walked home together.

He saw what was in her hand. "Is that an invitation to our fair?" he asked.

"Yes," she said.

"What are you going to do with it?" he asked.

"I know what I'd *like* to do with it," she said. "I'd like to throw it away."

He looked surprised. "Why?" he asked.

"Because it's for Mrs. Peacham, that's why," said Nancy Ann. "The teacher says we should invite her because she's new here. I go past her house on the way home, so I have to give her this invitation and tell her about the fair!" Nancy Ann made a face.

"Don't you like her?" asked Michael.

"No, I don't," said Nancy Ann.

"But you don't even know her, do you?" asked Michael.

"I know her well enough," said Nancy Ann. "I went past her farm last month, and I thought I saw a pony. I went closer, and it *was* a pony, tied under an apple tree. I was going to pet her, and just then old Mrs. Peacham came running out of the house. She waved her arms and said, 'Stop. Don't take any of those apples!'"

"You weren't going to, were you?" asked Michael.

"Of course I wasn't," said Nancy Ann. "I told her I wasn't, and then I ran home."

"And now you have to go back," said Michael.

"Yes," said Nancy Ann. "I don't see why the teacher couldn't have asked someone else."

They came to Mrs. Peacham's farm. It was a small farm, with a house almost hidden by trees. A lane led to the house.

156

Michael waited while Nancy Ann went down the lane. The house was quiet. She stood on the porch for a little while, but she did not knock. She put the invitation down in front of the door. Then she tiptoed away.

She went back to the road. "There!" she said. "I left the invitation."

"Wasn't she at home?" asked Michael.

"I don't know," said Nancy Ann.

"I thought you were supposed to *give* her the invitation," said Michael. "I thought you were supposed to tell her about the fair."

"I was," said Nancy Ann, "but I didn't want her to come out and shout at me."

They walked down the road. Michael asked, "Did you promise the teacher to stop and tell Mrs. Peacham about the fair?"

Nancy Ann began to walk more slowly. "I did promise," she said. "I'd better go back."

"I'll go back with you," said Michael.

They went back to Mrs. Peacham's. They walked down the lane. The invitation was where Nancy Ann had left it. She picked it up and knocked at the door. Michael stood beside her.

A little old woman opened the door. She tipped her head to one side like a bird, and looked at them.

"I brought you this, Mrs. Peacham," said Nancy Ann. She held out the invitation.

Mrs. Peacham took it. "I can't read it without my glasses," she said.

"It's an invitation—to our fair at school," said Nancy Ann. "We're going to have an art show—and songs—and games."

"Didn't you come to see me one day?" asked Mrs. Peacham. "Didn't you run away before I could talk to you?"

"I—I didn't think you wanted me here," said Nancy Ann. "You thought I was taking your apples—and I wasn't. All I wanted was to see the pony."

"You didn't take any apples?" said Mrs. Peacham. "That's good, because they were green. I was afraid you might take a bite of a green apple and have a stomach-ache. There's nothing worse than a green-apple stomach-ache. But the apples are ripe now. Why don't you two go and pick some?"

"Thank you, we will," said Michael.

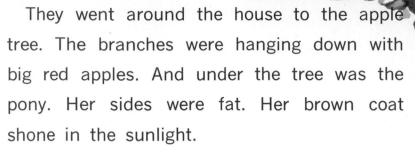

They went around the house to the apple tree. The branches were hanging down with big red apples. And under the tree was the pony. Her sides were fat. Her brown coat shone in the sunlight.

"Oh, she's beautiful!" said Nancy Ann.

"Her name is Tiny," said Mrs. Peacham. "Would you like to ride her?"

"Could we?" asked Nancy Ann.

"Yes," said Mrs. Peacham. "Just climb on. Tiny will know what to do."

Michael helped Nancy Ann up on the pony's back. The pony trotted around the apple tree. She ran in two neat circles before she stopped.

Then Michael took his turn.

"I used to keep ponies in the city," said Mrs. Peacham. "I used to run a pony ride in the park for boys and girls. But my rheumatism got worse. I couldn't help the boys and girls off and on any more, so I sold my ponies, all but Tiny. She was my favorite. When I came to the country to live, I just had to bring her with me."

"I'm sorry about your rheumatism," said Nancy Ann. "Will you be well enough to come to the fair?"

"I'm much better in the country," said Mrs. Peacham. "If I do come to the fair, could Tiny come? I think she misses the boys and girls. Besides, she needs exercise. You and your friends could have free rides."

"That would really be wonderful!" said Nancy Ann.

"Ask your teacher how she likes the idea," said Mrs. Peacham, "and let me know what she says."

"Our teacher will like it," said Michael. "She couldn't help liking it."

"Now," said Mrs. Peacham, "why don't we pick some apples?"

So they picked apples and sat under the tree to eat them.

"It's like a picnic," said Nancy Ann. "Here, Tiny, come to the picnic."

And the pony came straight to where they were sitting and joined the picnic, and ate an apple too.

Kangaroo Ride

I suppose it would be rather
  A risky thing to do,
But I'd like to go out riding
  On a leaping kangaroo!

I expect it would be bumpy
  Each time he touched the ground,
And hard to keep from slipping,
  With every lengthy bound;

But I shouldn't mind the jolting,
  Or having people stare,
With Australian towns behind me,
  And cool wind in my hair!

—*Elaine V. Emans*

Read the Signs

Signs help us and are needed for our safety. Below are signs that may help Gus, Danny, or you. See if you can tell which signs would be used by Gus in the water, Danny in the orchard, or you on the way to school.

Make other signs that Gus, Danny, or you might need. Then ask a friend to tell who would use the signs.

Make Up a Name

When a new machine is made, a new name has to be thought of for it. *Shellaphone* was a new machine made by Jack Eel. You can tell where the name *Speedmobile* came from. Look at the picture below.

What is happening in the picture? What is a good name for this machine?

What is a good name for a machine that spreads jam on bread?

What name would you give a machine that can cut and paste at the same time?

What is a good name for a machine that picks up apples and puts them in boxes?

Draw a picture of a new machine and think of a name for it.

The World Around Us

THINK AND TRY

We were ready for supper.

Dad dipped hot soup into our soup bowls. Dad was in a hurry to eat because he had an evening class. Just then Mom got a phone call.

Dad asked the blessing. I drank my milk and ate my soup. Dad ate and then he cleared the table and I helped him wash dishes. We left Mom's soup in the bowl on the table.

Dad finished grading some papers and then he grabbed his coat and rushed off to teach his evening class.

My mom and dad are teachers. They teach science, and sometimes we talk things over. But they won't answer some of my questions about science. They always say, "Think and try."

When Mom was finally able to come to the table she tasted her soup. She made a funny face. "Too cold," she said, and warmed it in the microwave oven. Then she ate it.

I did my homework. It was still early enough that I had some time to think, so I said to myself, "How come Mom's soup got cold? I'll think up some experiments and see if I can find out."

At our school the next day my friend Gina sat near me at lunch. We eat our lunches outside and sometimes it gets hot out there.

Gina likes milk. I do too. We buy cartons of milk for lunch at school. I like my milk good and cold. So I drink it right away.

Gina pours her milk into a saucer, which she brings in her lunch box every day. The milk sits in the saucer while Gina eats. "I let my milk warm up," she always says.

Here was a funny thing! My dad dipped hot soup into a bowl and it cooled off. Gina pours cold milk into a saucer, and it warms up. "What's going on here?" I say to myself. "Has this anything to do with science?"

I talked to Mom and Dad about it after school.

"What's going on with Mom's hot soup and Gina's cold milk?" I asked. "Anything to do with science?"

Dad winked. "Think and try," he said.

So I did. Mom helped me pour some hot water into a bowl. I put some cold water into a saucer, and added some food coloring to it—color for cold. And then I waited.

I worked with Tricks, my Scotty dog. She goes to Obedience School and is learning to sit when I say, "Sit." It is hard work.

"How about that hot and cold water?" Dad called after a bit.

So I tried to find out. I put my finger into the bowl. The hot water was not too hot, but it was not really cold.

I put my finger into the cold colored water and swished it around. I made small waves.

"How about it?" Mom asked.

"Oh," I said. "Funny thing. The cold water isn't so cold now and the hot water isn't very hot. Each one is sort of cool."

Mom and Dad laughed. "Sort of?" they called.

"Well, the saucer of colored water is cool," I called back. "The bowl of plain water feels warm, but it doesn't sting."

Mom and Dad came out to look. Dad didn't try either one. He just said, "Maybe you have something here."

I wanted to be sure. So I dumped the water into the sink. Then I saw Mom looking at the bowl and the saucer. It made me wonder. I looked at them too.

"Guess I'll try something new," I said.

"What?" Mom asked.

"Guess," I said. I didn't want to tell them. So Mom and Dad had to wait too.

I asked for some more hot water, but I didn't use the bowl. Saucers were more fun. I took two saucers this time. I put cold water and food coloring into a saucer. Then Mom poured the hot water into the other saucer.

"I am going to leave them here all night," I said.

Tricks went to bed and so did I. Sometimes Tricks sleeps in my room on her own blanket. This was one of those times. I always sleep better when Tricks is snoring nearby. I guess she sleeps better too.

We were the last ones up for breakfast.

Mom was fixing the sandwiches for lunch. Dad was eating scrambled eggs. And my two saucers were sitting there on the kitchen table.

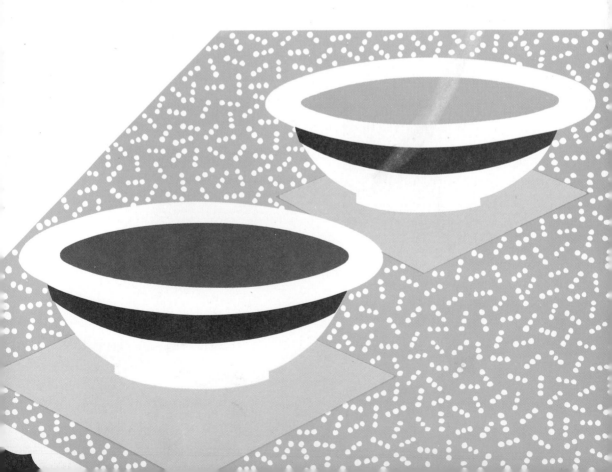

I put my finger into the saucer of colored water and made small waves with it. It felt just right for swimming. I put a finger of my other hand into the saucer of plain water. At last I understood.

I looked at Mom and Dad, and they were looking at me.

"It's something to do with science," I told them. "Think and try."

And Mom said, "We did. That's how we know."

So now the three of us know the answer. Do you?

DIPPY'S DAY
BY MOONLIGHT

It was evening on the desert. A full moon was rising. Dippy's day was just coming.

Desert sand in the daytime is too hot for a kangaroo rat like Dippy. He covers the openings of his house with dirt and sleeps in one room all day.

Night was daytime for Dippy. He woke up and stretched. He hopped around on his long hind legs to open the doors of his burrow.

That was easy! He just kicked aside little piles of dirt and let the moonlight come into the burrow.

175

Then he sat in a doorway on his hind legs and cleaned himself the way a cat does. He cleaned behind his ears. He smoothed his white front hairs and the tan fur on his back. He did not skip over his short front legs. When he finished, even the tuft of fur on his tail was fluffy and clean.

Breakfast came next. His little feet had made tiny tracks to nearby bushes. Dippy hopped off to them now. He sat up on his hind legs in front of some fat seeds and balanced himself with his long tail. With his front paws he brushed seeds from the stems into his open mouth.

A twig cracked close by! Dippy jumped ten feet. He changed his direction in midair. With zigzag leaps he reached the nearest hole into his burrow.

Inside he stopped, balanced himself, and trembled. His black eyes were wide open as he peeked out. A snake was going into the burrow of a neighbor rat, but Dippy was safe.

He stopped trembling and listened to other sounds. His ears spun around in different directions. Sand grains were blowing in the wind, and the full moon was higher. No snakes were near.

Dippy leaped to a spot of moonlight and froze again. Overhead an owl swished by, but it missed Dippy. Some other kangaroo rat might not be so lucky!

Dippy jumped to a clump of grasses. His front paws held some stems while his sharp teeth cut them off. He put them down to dry in a hollow of sand. He went from clump to clump, gathering his food and putting it to dry in the hollow.

It was hard work and his fur was full of dirt. He found a few seeds to eat, and then he headed for a bath in a dust hole.

It was just a hollow in the sand, but Dippy tested it well. There were tracks of birds and other animals all around it. There were some kangaroo-rat tracks too. This must be a favorite dust hole for a good bath.

Dippy hopped back to a nearby shadow. He looked and listened and waited. Nothing came to bother him, and into the dust hole he leaped.

He rolled around on his back in the hollow. He twisted and wiggled and turned. The dust was his bath water. It worked its way all through his fur and got rid of insects and twigs and dirt. It felt good!

Dippy finished his bath and jumped back to the shadow to brush himself. His white and tan fur was soon smooth again. The tuft on the end of his tail was fluffy.

A twig snapped, and Dippy zigzagged with big hops to get away from some new danger. Trembling, he waited until the desert was quiet, and looked around with his bright black eyes.

He saw kangaroo rats in the moonlight. They were playing tag and leapfrog on a sand hill, so he played with them.

All at once an owl hooted. Each rat leaped to his own burrow. A high scream told Dippy that one rat had not leaped fast enough.

A breeze carried the scent of ripe seeds to Dippy, and he was really hungry. He found some and ate a few. Then he filled his cheek pouches with some. His cheek pouches were fur-lined, a good basket for his seeds.

He carried them to a soft spot in the sand. He hid them in a little hollow and covered them. Back he went for more, always following the scent.

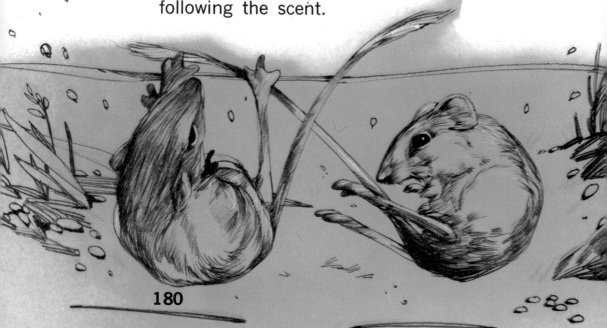

But another kangaroo rat was already stuffing his cheek pouches with seeds. Dippy leaped at him and landed, back to back, against the other rat. They kicked hard with their hind feet, and the sand flew in all directions. Each rat tried to keep his balance, but Dippy was bigger. One kick landed in the right spot. Over went the other rat. He rolled over and over, and Dippy chased him away.

Dippy went back to gather his seeds, but they were gone. Another rat had helped himself while Dippy was fighting.

His moonlight day was almost over, and he lost no time. He sat up on his hind legs and his nose twitched.

The right scent came, and he found more seeds. He ate some and then filled his cheek pouches. This time he took the seeds into his own burrow and stored them.

Daylight was coming. Dippy ate his supper and pushed dirt into each door of his burrow. He went into his sleeping room. He turned around and covered his nose with the fur tuft on his tail. One more wonderful day by moonlight was over, and it was bedtime for Dipodomys,[1] the little kangaroo rat of the desert.

[1] Dipodomys (digh·PO·də·mis)

182

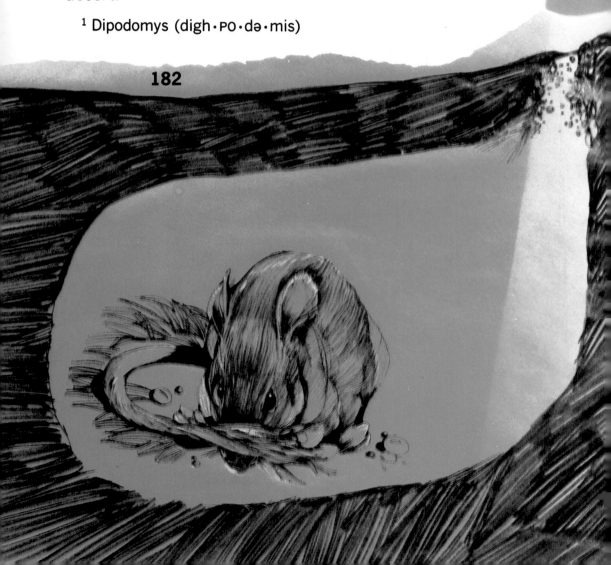

Rhyme

I like to see a thunder storm,
  A dunder storm,
    A blunder storm,
I like to see it, black and slow,
Come stumbling down the hills.

I like to hear a thunder storm,
  A plunder storm,
    A wonder storm,
Roar loudly at our little house
And shake the window sills!

—Elizabeth Coatsworth

183

WHERE IS WATER?

Everyone knows the answer to that question. When rain falls, we see water in puddles. Sometimes water rushes down the side of a mountain, carrying rocks with it. In a quiet lake, water is like a mirror. You can see the sky reflected in it.

Water floats leaves and little sticks in a running river. Sometimes there is so much water that it floods the land. At the seashore great waves of water come in from the ocean. They rise in a tower of foam and fall back into the ocean again.

Sometimes water is not so easy to see. It is inside plants and animals. It is in all of us. Did you know that you are made mostly of water?

Water is almost everywhere. It spreads out when we spill it. It soaks into things. It may be flowing into a lake at one spot and quietly flowing out at another. It fills low places.

Water is liquid. It can be clean enough to drink or it can be full of mud and dirt. It can also be salty, as it is in the ocean.

Water will not burn. It can help to put out fires.

Wonderful, wonderful water!

Yes, it is a liquid. But is it always a liquid?

Doesn't running water change when cold, cold winter comes? Is water always a liquid then?

When it gets very cold, water has another form. It turns to ice. When ice is thick enough, you can run over it and skate on it.

Ice is water in its solid form. So is hail that pelts down in round, hard balls.

Glaciers and icebergs are water in this solid form. Have you ever seen a glacier? Most glaciers are in high mountains. The ice in glaciers moves so slowly that you cannot see it move. But it does move. A mountain glacier is a solid river of snowy ice, that may move one inch in one day!

If the lower end of the glacier reaches the sea, great blocks of ice break off into the water. They are icebergs.

Snow is water in its solid form, because snow is made of delicate crystals of ice.

Where do snow crystals come from? And raindrops? And clouds? Where does the water they are made of come from? Do you ever wonder about that?

Here is one way to help you find out. Put a few drops of water in a saucer. Leave it there for a day or so. Then look at it again. The water is gone. It has gone into the air but you cannot see it there.

Lakes and oceans are like giant saucers that never dry up. So there must be lots of water in the air all the time.

187

Do you think this is where raindrops come from ? And snow ? And clouds ?

There is another way you may find out if water is really in the air. On a cold winter day, stand near a cold windowpane. Blow out a big breath of air against the glass. Do it again and again.

A foggy spot will come on the glass. Small drops of water will start to run down it. They were not there before you blew on the glass.

This form of water is in the air all the time. It was in your breath and you could not see it. Sneaky, isn't it ?

This is the third form of water. It is water vapor. Clouds and snow and raindrops all come from water vapor in the air.

Rain and snow and hail always fall. Rivers always run downhill. How does water get back up to make more rain and snow and hail ?

Do you ever wonder about that ?

189

The Lesser Light

Do you ever play in the moonlight? Do you ever talk about what the moon looks like to you?

For ages people have asked questions about the moon. Some believed it was a spinning ball of fire. Others thought it was a mirror that reflected the earth's lands and seas.

This "lesser light to rule the night" (Genesis 1:16) was a great mystery.

What does the moon look like to you as it rides along in the sky?

The moonlight seems to be brighter sometimes than others. A few days each month the moon is bright enough to let you see outdoors at night. Sometimes you can even read large print or tell colors.

The moonlight seems to be brighter some places than others. Away from city lights the moon and stars both seem to be brighter.

One evening one of the astronauts who went to the moon stood in front of his house with his wife. They were looking at the moon. "It doesn't seem possible that I stood up there on the moon. But I did. There were rocks and sand under my feet. There were craters falling away before me, and mountains towering about me."

Space flights and moon landings have given many facts about the moon. By going to the moon, man has solved some of the mysteries about the sun and the moon and the stars.

Moon Shadows

All kinds of stories are made up about the shadows on the moon. Many people talk about "the man in the moon" because some of the shadows make them think of a man's face. Look at the many "faces" of the moon and try to understand how people see something like that.

Before astronauts went to the moon some people said the "moon is made of green cheese." They meant that it looked to them as if it had holes in it.

However, the facts that astronauts and scientists tell us now, give us a better idea about what the moon is like.

Some day a spaceship may take you to the moon. You may really sit on it and take pictures of its mountains, or measure its big holes, called craters. Then you can zoom home to tell us what you found. Before you go, you should know some things.

The moon is our nearest neighbor in space. It has flat places, high pointed mountains, and wide craters.

There is no air on the moon. There are no clouds, no wind, no rain. So there is no water. There are no rivers, no oceans.

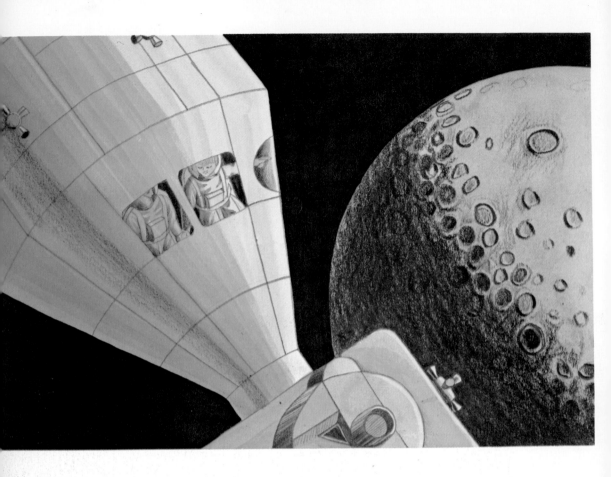

You will see stars in the daytime, if you go
to the moon. They will be clear bright points
of light, and the sky will be dark.

When we see the full moon rise in the sky,
it glows with light. The moon looks like a
shining silver ball, doesn't it? But the moon
has no light of its own.

Where does the shining light on the moon's face come from? It comes from the sun and is reflected from the face of the moon.

Where there are mountains on the moon's face, the light makes shadows. They always point away from the sun.

Scientists look at pictures of the moon's shadows and measure them.

These scientists can measure how high the mountains are by their shadows. When the mountains are very high, the shadows are long and shaped like ice cream cones.

In these shadows the moon is colder than anything we know on the earth.

The pictures also show big craters on the moon. Scientists think that one of the craters may be 140 miles wide!

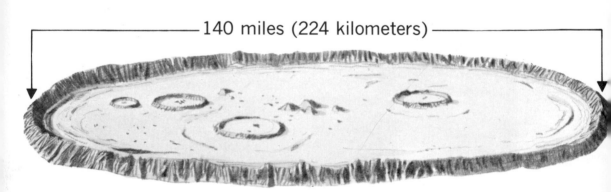

140 miles (224 kilometers)

Shadows tell us about the craters. They show that there are rings of mountains around these big holes. There are also mountains in the centers of some craters.

The moon shows us many "faces" as it rides along in the sky. It may be a thin crescent of light. It may look like a big letter D. The crescents, the letter D, and the full moon all reflect light from the sun.

Shadows have all kinds of stories to tell. Some day we may know even more about the moon. Scientists are busy finding out.

But best of all, the moon may be one of the places we can visit when God makes this earth new and there is no more sin.

THE EARTH OUR HOME

The Earth is our home. What sort of home it is depends on how we treat it, just as the houses we live in depend on how we take care of them.

Do you like to watch fish swim? Do you like to walk or ride through the woods? Do you like to breathe fresh air? Or to watch birds and hear them sing?

If you do, we'll all have to treat our Earth home in a different way. Why?

Because we are making lakes and rivers too dirty for fish to live in or for boys and girls to swim in.

Because we're cutting down our forests too fast, we are spoiling the countryside.

Because we're making so much smoke, dirty air often hides the sky and even nearby things. The dirty air makes it hard for us to breathe, and it makes our eyes water.

Because we're putting so much poison on the things birds eat, they are finding it hard to live.

Because we throw away things we do not want or need, we litter our streets and highways.

There are many things we do to live, to keep warm, and to move about that spoil the earth, the air, and the water.

Have you seen smoke pouring out of tall factory chimneys? Have you smelled the gas fumes from the back of a bus? Have you noticed the smoke from a jet plane taking off? All of these things make the air dirty—they pollute it.

Have you seen dirty streams pouring from factories? Have you wondered where the sewage from one house, many houses, a big city goes? It pollutes rivers and lakes and may even make them die. Fish can't live in them, and you can't swim in them. Even the ocean is getting a little sick.

Have you wondered where the wood for houses comes from? And the paper for books and newspapers? From our forests. And what does the land look like when the trees are gone?

Have you thought where the poison goes that we spray on gardens and grass to kill insects and weeds? Onto the things the birds eat, making it hard for them to live and share with us their beautiful colors and songs.

Have you seen piles of old cars and old refrigerators? Not very nice to look at, are they? Have you seen piles of old boxes, glass jars, and cans? Not very beautiful, are they?

If we don't do anything about this spoiling of the world around us—its air, its water, its land, and its life—our lives are not going to be so nice. But there is much that we can do.

201

Factories can clean their smoke. Cars and planes can be made so that their fumes do not add to the pollution.

The dirty water from factories can be made clean. Sewage, too, can be changed so that water is clean enough to use again. Fish can live again, and you can swim again in oceans, rivers, and lakes.

The mountains can still be covered with forests if the cutting of trees is done with care. We must plant again where we have cut. And we can have enough wood for houses and paper for books.

Many of the things we use are worn out and cannot be used any more. But they do not have to be left around. We can change many things back into what they were made of, and use them again. Old newspapers can become new paper. Old glass jars can be turned into new glass. Old iron can help to make new cars and refrigerators.

We can also learn not to litter. We all know the sign: DO NOT LITTER. But not everyone does what the sign says.

For a long time, people have used their Earth home without thinking of what was happening to it. Now we see that we must treat it better if it is to be a nice home. It can be.

Solid, Liquid, or Vapor?

Which things are solid?
Which things are liquid?
Which things are vapor?

Classifying items into three groups or classes

Science Experiments

1. Put a small pan of water in a sunny window. Put another small pan of water away from the sunshine. What happened to the water after two days? Which pan became empty first? Why?

2. Hang a wet towel in the classroom in the morning. In the late afternoon feel the towel. What happened? Where did the water go?

3. Remove the labels from two soup cans. Paint one can black and the other white. Put a thermometer in each can. Place them in a sunny window. Wait a few hours and check the temperature. Which can had the higher temperature? What have you learned about color and heat?

4. Place a plant on a windowsill in the sun. After two days look at the plant carefully. How has it changed? Which way did the plant lean? Now turn the plant around and check it again in two days. What happened? Why?

Once There Was

Little Robert Hare

A ship set sail from Ireland,
   In 1863.
The wind pushed out its mighty sails
   And took it out to sea.

The ship was full of pioneers
   Who'd left their homes behind,
To go out to New Zealand,
   A better place to find.

Behind them stood their empty barns.
   No food grew in the land.
Their plows lay broken in the fields.
   Clouds darkened Ireland.

Of all the people on that ship
     None had a better plan,
Than did the preacher Joseph Hare,
     And his big family clan.

Each night at sea the Hares would meet
     For talk and prayer and song.
"I know it's hard," said Father Hare,
     "And that the trip is long.

"But in New Zealand there will be
     God's work for us to do.
"You each will have a share in it.
     Yes. Everyone of you."

As Father Hare spoke to his ten,
     'Twas little Robert Hare
Who pictured in his mind the place
     And wished most to be there.

"We're here! We're here!" called
    Robert Hare,
  As he looked all around.
He saw the tall and green pine trees,
  He saw the little town.

The little town of Kaeo looked
  Like pictures on a wall,
With trees, a church, a little store,
  And houses big and small.

The Hares camped out in three big tents
  Set side by side in line.
But soon they built their own fine house
  From strong New Zealand pine.

When Father Hare preached at the Church,
  The people came to hear.
The Hares made friends with everyone
  Who came from far and near.

Each one of the Hare children had
   A special job to do.
Young Robert watched the baby, Sam,
   And Sister Judy too.

The older boys worked at the mill.
   The rest helped here and there.
Their mother's love shone like the sun
   Around them everywhere.

Until the day, the sun went out,
   The day their mother died.
On that sad day the world was dark.
   Oh, how the children cried.

The next day Robert sat alone
  And thought a long, long time.
He thought sad thoughts, but then he said,
  "I think I'll try a rhyme."

So Robert Hare wrote his first poem
  About dear Mother Hare.
And with the words he tried to tell
  About her love and care.

When Robert's father read the poem
  To everyone that night,
His words and thoughts lit up the dark
  Just like a candle's light.

Camp Meeting Storyteller

One day Uriah was walking down the street. He saw a tall black woman coming toward him. Uriah waved. "Hello," he called.

Sojourner Truth waved to Uriah. "Hello, young man," she said. "What's that book you have under your arm?"

"It's my Bible," Uriah answered.

Uriah ran toward Sojourner. "Will you tell me a story?" he asked. "Tell me about the bad boys at camp meeting."

Sojourner put her hand on Uriah's head. "I've told you that story before," she said. "You want to hear it again?"

Uriah nodded his head. "Yes," he said. "It's a good story."

"Well," Sojourner said. "I'll tell you the story. But I want you to do something for me too."

"I'll be glad to," said Uriah. "What can I do?"

Sojourner reached out and touched Uriah's Bible. "Read to me. I want to hear the story of Jesus again."

Uriah smiled, "That's a good story too," he said. "I'll go tell my mother where I'm going. Then I'll come to your house."

When Uriah got to Sojourner's house she was sitting on a chair. She looked very old and tired. But when she saw Uriah she sat up straight and started her story.

"It was late in the evening. The moon was shining on the tents and the preacher was preaching about Jesus," she said. "Everything was quiet and the people were all listening."

"But it didn't stay quiet for long," Uriah said.

"That's right," said Sojourner. "I think you know this story better than I do. Maybe I'll just stop telling it."

"No, I want to hear you tell it. Tell me more," said Uriah.

"There were some boys who thought it would be fun to stop the camp meeting. They came to the tents and shouted. Then they started to shake the tent poles.

"Weren't you afraid?" asked Uriah.

"Yes, I was. Everyone was. But I prayed and I asked Jesus to go with me. Then I went outside the tent and looked around. There was a little hill not far from the tent. I walked over and climbed up on top of that hill. The boys ran over to see what I was going to do.

"I started to sing. The boys stood there with sticks in their hands. I was afraid they might hurt me. But they didn't. They just asked me to sing another song.

"I sang again. Then I started to talk to them. I told them that there were two kinds of people at the camp meeting—the sheep and the goats. The other preacher had the sheep and I had the goats.

"They all laughed, but they listened when I told them about Jesus. I talked, and talked, but I was getting tired. So I asked those boys to do something for me.

"I wanted them to go away. So I told them I was tired and I was only going to sing one more song. I asked them if they would go away while I sang.

"At first they didn't want to. But finally they said they would go. I started to sing. By the time I finished, they were all gone."

"I don't think I would have been able to sing," Uriah said. "I would have been so afraid I wouldn't have been able to open my mouth."

Sojourner smiled, "When the lions were all around Daniel, God shut the lions' mouths. But when those boys were all around me, God opened my mouth."

Uriah looked down at his Bible. "Well, I guess it's my turn," he said. "What story would you like me to read?"

"Read about when Jesus went up on the mountain and preached to the people," Sojourner said. "I want to know what He said when He preached." She smiled. "Who knows, I might have to preach from the top of a hill again sometime."

Uriah opened his Bible and started to read.

The Warm Church

William Farnsworth was one of the first Seventh-day Adventists in the world. He had twenty-two children. This play is about two of them. It takes place a long time ago, in 1841.

Characters

Mother	Three men's voices
John, age 8	Father
Stephen, age 6	Uncle Dan
Aunt Mary	Grandpa

Part One

(A bedroom with a door and window. A big bed is by the door. A small table is by the bed. On the other side of the door are stairs going down to the living room door. **John** *and* **Stephen** *are in bed.* **Mother** *is standing at the door.)*

Mother: Go right to sleep, children. Father is having a special meeting downstairs. You are not to be seen or heard.

John: Yes, Mother.

Stephen: Yes, Mother.

*(***Mother*** goes out and shuts the door. She goes down the stairs into the living room. We can't see into the living room but the door to it is open a little bit.)*

Stephen: *(pokes* **John***)* Listen. *(They listen.)* That's Uncle Dan laughing. He and Aunt Mary must be downstairs.

John: Could be. I'm going to see what's going on.

(**John** *gets out of bed and tiptoes to the window.* **John** *makes a sign for* **Stephen** *to come to the window.* **Stephen** *jumps out of bed, making a noise as his feet hit the floor.*)

John: Be quiet, will you.

(**Stephen** *tiptoes over to the window, tries to see out.*)

Stephen: (*Runs and gets back in bed.*) You're the one who's going to get licked. Not me. I can't see out the window anyhow. It's too high.

(**Stephen** *pulls up the blanket. He closes his eyes tight.*)

John: (*looking out the window*) Why are so many people here? There's Grandpa's cart. Look at all the horses.

(**John** *turns from the window. Voices come from downstairs.*)

John: (*to himself*) What are they talking about? I just have to know what's going on.

(**John** *tiptoes to the door and quietly opens it. He turns and looks at* **Stephen** *in bed.* **John** *goes out the door, stands at the top of the stairs and looks down. Very quietly he tiptoes down one step, then another.*)

Man's Voice: (*from the living room*) This is a fine idea.

Older Man's Voice: (*from the living room*) My wife is going to be happy about this.

Another Man's Voice: (*from the living room*) We can finish it in three or four weeks. What do you say, neighbors? Shall we start at once? (*Everyone in the living room starts talking at once.*)

(**John** *takes another step down. Then* **Stephen**
comes rolling down the stairs, right at **John**.
John *tries to jump out of the way but trips
over* **Stephen**. *They roll down the last four
steps.* **Aunt Mary** *comes out of the living
room with a lighted candle and shuts the
door.*)

Aunt Mary: (*getting down on the floor*) Oh, boys! Are you hurt? Are you all right?

John: He tripped me. He can't do anything right.

Aunt Mary: Maybe not, but Stephen is very brave. See the tears in his eyes? But he didn't cry out.

(**John** *looks at* **Stephen** *who is rubbing his knee.*)

John: I'm sorry, Stephen. I'm sorry you're hurt. It's all because of me. I should have stayed in bed. Here, let me help you.

(**John** *and* **Aunt Mary** *help* **Stephen** *up the stairs.* **Aunt Mary** *puts the candle by the bed. She helps the boys get back into bed, then she sits on the bed.*)

Aunt Mary: Let me take a look at you. (*She looks at their arms, faces, and feet.*)

Stephen: (*more afraid than hurt*) Did anyone hear us, Aunt Mary?

Aunt Mary: I think I was the only one. I was sitting by the door. Well, nothing is broken. You'll be all right.

John: Who are all those people, Aunt Mary? What are they doing here? Please tell us.

Aunt Mary: Well, they're the farmers from around here. They are talking about building a church—our own church—and it will be nearby. It's such a long way to the church in town. It's hard for the mothers and babies.

Stephen: It's hard for me too. It's so cold in the church and the preacher talks on and on. I hope they put a great big stove in the new church. I hope the preacher won't talk so long.

John: Oh Stephen! That's no way to talk. Take back what you said.

Stephen: No. I won't take it back. You know you wish it too. You know you do.

John: (*thinking*) Well. I—I guess so.

Aunt Mary: (*Getting up from the bed and speaking softly.*) Good night, boys. You'd better go to sleep. (*Picks up the candle.*) And I'd better go back downstairs.

(**Aunt Mary** *goes downstairs.* **Stephen** *and* **John** *go to sleep.*)

Part Two
The next morning.

(*The downstairs living room. A big table with chairs is in the middle of the room. A window is behind the table. A door leads to the outside on one wall. Another door is on the other side.* **Father** *is at the table, reading a sheet of paper.* **Mother** *is sitting beside him. Food is on the table and four places are set.*)

Father: Well, Mother. All the farmers signed their names. All thirty-two. It looks like we are going to have our new church.

Mother: Yes. I'm so happy about it.

Father: (*Puts down the paper and looks at the table.*) Now, where are the boys? They are sleeping very late this morning.

Mother: They are coming. They went to sleep late.

(**Stephen** *and* **John** *come rushing in.*)

Father: Well, there you are. Come on. Sit down and eat.

(*The boys sit down at their places and* **Mother** *helps them get their food.*)

Father: What's this I hear about you boys going to sleep late last night?

(**Stephen** *and* **John** *look at each other, then at* **Mother**.)

Mother: Now, Father. There were a lot of people here last night and a lot of talking.

Father: You're right about that, Mother. (*He smiles and turns to the boys.*) I was once a boy myself. I remember what it was like to be in bed and hear people talking.

Mother: Tell them, Father.

Father: Oh, yes. Boys, we're going to build a new church right near here. That's what the meeting was about. (*He picks up the paper.*) Thirty-two farmers signed their names on this paper. They are all going to help build the church.

Mother: Each family is going to give something to the church.

Father: Uncle Dan and Grandpa will be here soon. We're going to the mill for lumber.

John: But what about us?

Stephen: Yes. Can't we help too?

Father: That's just what I was coming to. I want you boys to go with us. You can help load the lumber onto the wagons and . . .

Stephen: Can we help drive the horses?

Father: Of course, of course!

John: I want to help build!

Stephen: Me, too!

(*The sound of horses arriving.* **Stephen** *and* **John** *go to the window.*)

Stephen and John: It's Grandpa, Uncle Dan, and Aunt Mary. They're here!

Father: (*Opens the door.*) Good morning. Come on in.

(**Grandpa, Aunt Mary** *and* **Uncle Dan** *come in. Family members say "Good morning," "How are you today," "I'm so happy to see you."*)

Aunt Mary: (*She stands by* **John** *and* **Stephen**.) Well, boys. Is everything all right this morning?

Stephen: Oh, yes, Aunt Mary.

John: We're going to help Father and Uncle Dan and Grandpa.

Stephen: We're going to help drive the horses . . .

John: And load the wagons . . .

Stephen: And build the church.

Uncle Dan: (*to* **John** *and* **Stephen**) What's this I hear about a stove, and the preacher not talking so long?

Father: A stove, you say?

Uncle Dan: Why yes, William. Mary told me. . . .

Aunt Mary: Let them tell us, Dan. Let the boys speak.

Grandpa: That's what I say. Sit down everyone so we can hear what these young ones have to say.

(*Everyone sits down.* **Stephen** *and* **John** *stand side by side. They look at each other. They look at* **Mother**, *at* **Father**, *at* **Aunt Mary**.)

Father: It's all right. Speak up now.

Mother: Go on, boys.

John: Well, . . . (*to* **Stephen**) You say it.

Stephen: It's so cold in the church. Please put a big stove in the new church. Make it a warm church.

John: And the preacher talks too long. We don't know what all the words mean.

(*No one speaks.* **John** *and* **Stephen** *run to* **Mother** *and hide their heads in her arms.*)

Grandpa: I told you to listen to those young ones.

Father: (*Going over to* **John** *and* **Stephen** *and taking them by the hand.*) Those are mighty fine ideas you boys have. You are going to have your stove. You can even help pick it out.

Stephen: Really?

John: We can?

Father: That's what I said. And we will make sure the preacher doesn't talk too long.

Uncle Dan: How about a Sabbath School for the children, William, with their own teacher.

Aunt Mary: I'd like to be the teacher.

Stephen: Oh, boy!

John: You would, Aunt Mary?

Aunt Mary: I sure would.

Father: Amen. So be it. Come on now, everyone get to work. No more talk. Let's get busy and start building the new church.

Mother: The new *warm* church!

*(Everyone laughs. **Mother** and **Aunt Mary** help the boys put on their coats. **Father, Uncle Dan,** and **Grandpa** go out. **John** and **Stephen** run after them. **Mother** and **Aunt Mary** wave from the door and window.)*

So everyone helped and the church was built in just four weeks. A great big stove warmed the church. There were meetings for the children and the preacher didn't talk too long. The church later became the first Seventh-day Adventist Church in the world, and Adventists still meet there. The picture below shows the church as it is today. William Farnsworth and members of his family are buried in the churchyard where they wait for Jesus to come.

THE ISLAND

They mowed the meadow down below
Our house the other day
But left a grassy island where
We still can go and play.

Right in the middle of the field
It rises green and high;
Bees swing on the clover there,
And butterflies blow by.

This island is a far-off place
With oceans all around.
The only thing to see is sky,
And wind, the only sound.

—Dorothy Aldis

Sarah Decides

(A story from long ago)

Sarah Cunningham could not sit still. She wiggled around on the seat of the buggy. "Are we there yet?" she asked her father.

Father smiled. "It won't be much longer," he said. "We should see the camp meeting tents soon."

"I don't care about seeing the tents," Sarah said. "I just want to see my friends Emily and Dan and John and Jennifer and . . ."

Father laughed. "You will see them. But do you know who else will be here?"

"Who?" Sarah asked. "Will there be a new family?"

"Well, yes," Father answered. "Elder and Mrs. White will be here."

Sarah stopped wiggling. She sat on the edge of her seat with her eyes wide open. "You mean I'm going to see Mrs. White?"

"Yes, you will," Father said. "She will speak at the children's meetings and you might even get to talk to her."

Sarah was early for the first meeting. She picked a seat near the middle of the tent and waited for the meeting to start.

Soon Sarah saw Mrs. White. "She looks so happy," Sarah said to the girl sitting beside her. "Look how she smiles all the time."

The meeting began with some songs and then Mrs. White stood up.

Mrs. White talked about Jesus and His love for children. Then she asked the children if they would like to know Jesus better. "If you love Jesus and would like to be a Christian, come to these seats in the front row," she said.

The children started to wiggle. They looked down at their feet. Many were thinking that they loved Jesus and would like to learn more about Him. But they did not want to get up in front of all of their friends and walk to the front row.

"I'll wait until someone else goes first," Sarah thought. Then she looked up and saw Mrs. White smiling. "Mrs. White knows Jesus so well," Sarah said to herself. "I want to know Him too. I can't wait for everyone else to decide. I'll just get up and go."

As Sarah got out of her seat and started toward the front row, she could feel everyone looking at her. But she didn't mind. She had decided to be a Christian. Jesus had died for her. Walking to the front of the tent was just a little thing to do for Him.

Sarah sat down. Mrs. White talked to her. Soon other children were coming. Mrs. White talked with them too.

All that week Elder and Mrs. White helped the children learn what the Bible says about Jesus. By the end of the week, several children had decided to be baptized.

Sarah liked learning more about Jesus. She wanted to be baptized too, but she was afraid of the water. When she got near water, her hands got cold and she couldn't talk.

Sarah talked to Mrs. White. "I want to be baptized," she said. "But I am afraid of the water."

Mrs. White said, "Friday we will baptize those who have decided to live for Jesus. You must come. Jesus will help you get over your fear."

Friday morning Sarah felt all kinds of things mixed up inside her. She felt light and happy. Today she was giving her life to Jesus. But way down in her stomach was a cold hard feeling. She was still afraid of the water.

In the afternoon she went to the lake. Her mother and father went with her. Nine other girls were getting ready to be baptized. Sarah turned away. Her shoulders shook. She couldn't even look at the other girls going into the water.

Then Sarah felt a hand on her shoulder. She looked up. Mrs. White was smiling at her.

"Here, Sarah," Mrs. White said. "Let me help you get your robe on." Sarah tried to smile as Mrs. White helped her.

Then Mrs. White took her hand and Sarah started toward the water. Mrs. White bent down and got a little water in her hands. She put some water on Sarah's hands and a little on her head.

"You see, the water will not hurt you," she said. "You have decided to give your life to Jesus. He will keep you safe."

Sarah felt something come loose inside her. The cold hard feeling in her stomach was gone. Slowly she walked out into the water and let Elder White baptize her.

After she came up from the water she looked toward Mrs. White. She was smiling. Sarah smiled a big smile and walked out of the water.

"I am so glad you have decided to live for Jesus," Mrs. White said. "Today you have told Jesus that you will go where He wants you to go."

"Thank you," Sarah said. "Thank you for helping me to know Jesus better. Now I know that He will go everywhere with me. With Jesus I don't have to be afraid."

243

Write a Story of Long Ago

Now that you have read about Adventists of long ago, here are some things you should know about another one.

Mary Andrews was 13 years old when she went to Switzerland with her brother, Charles, and her father, John Nevins Andrews. They were the first Seventh-day Adventist missionaries to go to Switzerland. They left Boston in 1874 on a ship. Mary's mother had died just two years before.

Think about the stories you have read about early Adventists. Remembering these stories might help you imagine what Mary may have been thinking and doing on her trip from Boston to Switzerland. Working together with other children and your teacher, make up a story about Mary and her trip. You may want to make it into a book with drawings. Or you may decide to act it out as a play or a puppet show.

The Road to Heaven

The early Adventists you have read about all hoped to see Jesus some day. Follow the road to heaven. Tell each story as you come to a picture.

Girls Can Be Anything

by Norma Klein

"Now we will play hospital," said Adam Sobel. "I will be the doctor and you will be the nurse."

Adam Sobel was Marina's best friend in her class. They went home on the bus together and at school, in the yard, they sat and pretended to fish. They were the only ones in the class who could do the lion puzzle and get all the pieces of the mane together. Usually Marina liked the games Adam thought up, but this time she said, "I want to be the doctor too."

"You can't be doctor if *I'm* doctor," Adam said.

"Why not?" said Marina.

"There can't be two doctors," Adam said.

"So, *you* be the nurse and *I'll* be the doctor," Marina said.

"That's not the way it goes," Adam said. He was already putting on the white doctor coat that was with the clothes in the "play" box. "Girls are always nurses and boys are always doctors."

"Why is that?" said Marina.

"That's just the way it is," Adam said. "Could I have the stethoscope, please, Nurse?"

That night Marina told her father at dinner, "I don't like Adam Sobel at all."

"Oh?" Father said. "I thought he used to be your favorite."

"He used to be," Marina said, "but you know what he said today?"

"What?" asked Father.

"He said girls can't be doctors. They have
to just be nurses."

"Well, that's just plain silly!" her father
said. "Of *course* they can be doctors."

"They can?" asked Marina.

"Certainly they can," Father replied. "Why your Aunt Rosa is a doctor. You know that."

"But is she a real one?" Marina said.

"She sure is, as real as they come," Father said.

"Does she work in a hospital and wear a white uniform?" Marina wanted to know.

"She does," Father said. "In fact, she works in the very hospital where you were born. You know what she does there?"

"What?" said Marina.

"She's a surgeon," Father said. "She takes out tonsils. That's hard work, you know."

The next day at school, Marina said to Adam, "I have an aunt who's a doctor. She's a surgeon."

"Is she a real doctor?" Adam wanted to know.

"Of *course* she's real," Marina said. "She comes to our house for dinner. She even has a white uniform. . . . Lots of women are doctors. I might be one. I might be one that takes care of animals.

"I could have my own hospital and dogs and cats would come to see me and I would make them better," Marina said. "That's the kind of doctor I want to be."

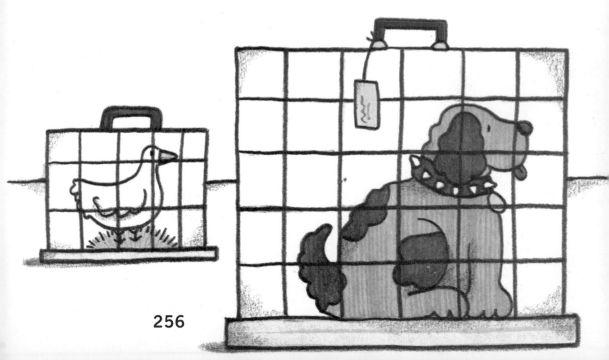

"I don't want to *be* a doctor," Adam said.

"What do you want to be?" asked Marina.

"I think I want to be a pilot," Adam said.

"You mean, you'd have your own airplane and fly it from place to place?"

"Yes," Adam said. "Why don't we play airplane right now?"

258

"O.K.," said Marina. "How do we do it?"

"Well," said Adam, "this is the plane and I sit in front flying."

"What do *I* do?" said Marina.

"You're the flight attendant," Adam said. "You walk around in back and give the people something to eat and drink."

So Marina poured some water in paper cups left over from juice time. She walked around and gave them to all the people. She always asked them first what they wanted. Finally, she went over to where Adam was and asked, "What are you doing?"

"I'm still flying the plane," Adam said. "Oh, oh—here we come. . . . It might be a crash landing. . . . Better look out."

"You know what?" Marina said.

"What?" said Adam, who was keeping his eyes on the place where the plane had to land.

"I think *I* want to be a pilot," Marina said.

"*You* can't be a pilot," Adam said.

"If I want to, I can," Marina said.

"Girls can't be pilots," Adam said. "They have to be flight attendants."

"But that's boring," said Marina. And she went off and began to drive her own pretend plane.

That night in bed Marina said to her mother, "Adam Sobel is so bad."

"Is he?" her mother said. "What did he do?"

"He said girls can't fly planes," Marina said. "He said they have to be flight attendants."

"Not always," Mother said.

"Then, how come he said it?" Marina asked.

"Maybe he didn't know," Mother answered. "There was a picture of a woman in the newspaper just the other day, and she's been flying her own plane for seventeen years."

"Does she fly with people in it?" Marina asked.

"Of course!" said Mother.

"Does she fly it all by herself?" Marina said.

"Well, she has a copilot," Mother said. "Pilots always have copilots to help them."

"Mommy?"

"Yes, darling."

"If I was a pilot, would you and Daddy fly with me in my plane?"

"We certainly would."

"Would I be a good pilot, do you think?" Marina asked.

"I think you would," Mother said.

The next day at school Marina told Adam, "Today you can be my copilot. I'm going to be a pilot like that lady in the paper who has her own plane."

"What lady is that?" Adam said.

"Oh, I guess you didn't see her picture," Marina said. "Her plane has people in it and everything. Even her mother and father fly in it with her."

"Who is the flight attendant in that plane?" Adam said.

"It's a self-service plane," Marina said. "In the back there's a little machine and you get your drinks by putting in money."

"That sounds like a good idea," Adam said.

He let Marina be pilot and he was copilot and read the map and told her where to go. There was almost a crash landing, but Marina landed in a grassy field and everyone got out safely.

That afternoon Mrs. Darling read the class a story about a king and queen. They wore long red robes and had yellow crowns on their heads.

On the way home in the bus Marina said, "How about being a king? Or a queen?"

Adam thought about that for a minute. "No."

"You could have a red robe," Marina said. "You could have a crown."

Adam shook his head. "That wouldn't be comfortable. Anyway, kings and queens don't *do* anything anymore. It would be boring."

"Maybe that's true," Marina said.

"What I'd like to be," Adam said, "is president. That's *better* than being a king."

"President of what?" Marina wanted to know.

"Just president."

"You mean *The* President?" Marina said.

"That's right," Adam said.

"What would you do if you were president?" Marina asked.

"Oh," answered Adam, "I would sit in a big room with a rug on the floor and a big desk and I would sign papers and everyone would have to do whatever I said."

"Maybe tomorrow we can play President," Marina said.

"O.K.," Adam said.

"Only, the thing is," Marina said, "what would I be while you were president?"

"You could be my wife."

"What would I do if I were your wife?" asked Marina.

"Well, you could cook dinner and get the newspaper ready when I got home," Adam said. "Sometimes you could ride in a car with me and we could wave at people and they would throw confetti at us."

"That sounds like fun," Marina said, "only, Adam?"

"Listen," Adam said. "One thing I *know*. There's *never* been a woman president."

That night after supper Marina said to her mother and father, "I don't know what we're going to *do* with Adam Sobel. He says such silly things."

"What did he say today that was so silly?" her father said.

"He said there never was a woman president," Marina said.

There was a pause.

"Isn't he a silly boy!" Marina said.

"Well, it's true, there's never been a woman President of the United States," Mother said.

"Have there been women presidents of other places?" said Marina.

"Other countries have had important women leaders," Father said. "Mrs. Ghandi in India. Mrs. Meir in Israel. Mrs. Thatcher in England."

The next morning Marina said to Adam, "Adam, you know, *you* can be a pilot or a doctor. You know what I'm going to be?"

"What?" Adam said.

"I'm going to be the first woman President! . . . You can be my husband."

"What would I do?" Adam said.

"You would fly our plane and fly me from place to place so I could give speeches," Marina said.

"It seems like according to you, girls can be anything they want," Adam said.

"Well, that's just the way it is now," Marina said. "Will you fly me to where I can give my talk?"

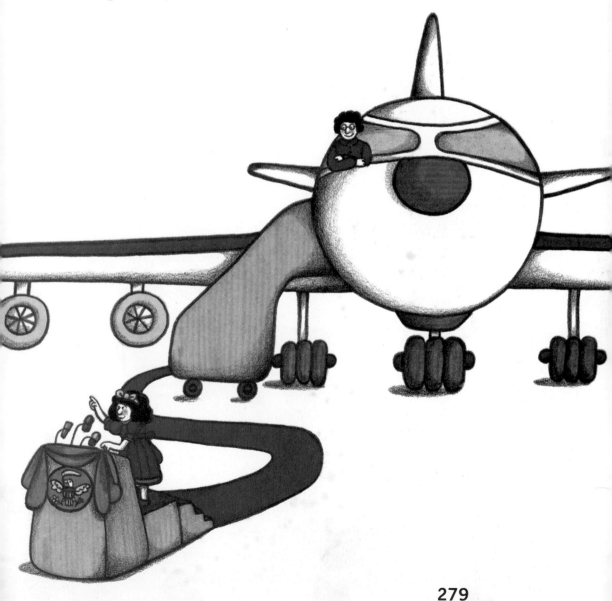

"O.K., but after you give your talk, you have to fly me back so I can give my talk," Adam said.

"O.K.," Marina said.

So Adam flew the plane to where Marina had to give her talk, and she gave it.

Then Marina flew Adam to where he had to give his talk, and he gave it.

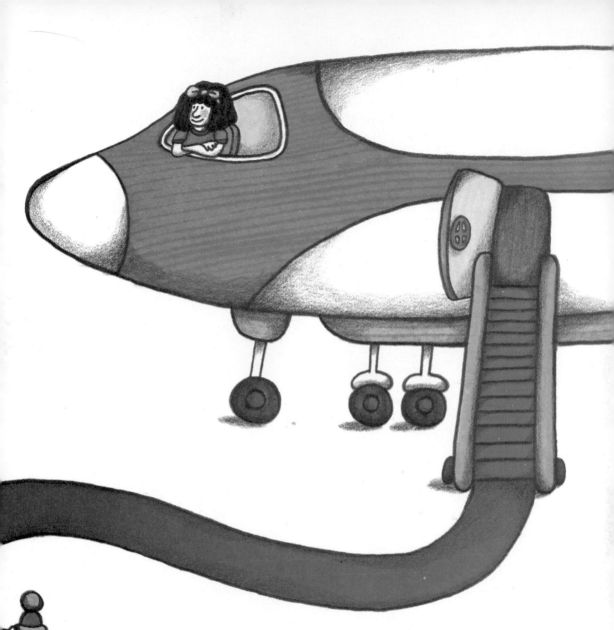

Then there was a big presidential dinner
with popcorn, apples, juice, and ice cream
for dessert.

Both Presidents thought it was delicious.

Key to Pronunciation

Letter Symbol for a sound	Key Word and Its Respelling	Letter Symbol for a sound	Key Word and Its Respelling
a	pat (PAT)	ch	church (CHERCH)
ah	far (FAHR)	hw	when (HWEN)
ai	air (AIR)	ks	mix (MIKS)
aw	jaw (JAW)	kw	quick (KWIK)
ay	pay (PAY)	ng	thing (THING)
e	pet (PET)		finger (FING-gər)
ee	bee (BEE)	sh	shoe (SHOO)
ehr	berry (BEHR-ee)	ss	case (KAYSS)
er	term (TERM)	th	thing (THING)
i	pit (PIT)	th	this (THIS)
igh	sigh (SIGH)	zh	pleasure (PLEZH-ər)
ihr	pier (PIHR)		
o	pot (POT)		
oh	oh, boat (BOHT)		
oi	oil (OIL)		
oo	boot, rule (ROOL)		
or	for (FOR)		
ow	power (POW-ər)		
u	put, book (BUK)		
uh	cut (KUHT)		

y	used in place of (igh) before two consonant letters as in child (CHYLD)
ə	represents the sound for any vowel spelling when a syllable is sounded very weakly, as in the first syllable of about, or the last syllables of item, gallop, or focus, or the middle syllable of charity

Glossary

add (AD) 1. To combine into a total; find the sum of: If you *add* 12 and 12, you get 24. 2. To state or write further: The guide completed his description of the park and *added* that maps were available at the ranger's office. **added, adding.**

aim (AYM) 1. Point or direct toward a target: He *aimed* his rifle at the bear. 2. An intention; purpose: Joe's *aim* in life is to be a preacher. **aimed, aiming.**

be·hold·en (bi-HOHL-dn) Owing a debt; obligated: They were *beholden* to the farmer for his help.

bound (BOWND) 1. Obliged, required: Jim is *bound* to repay the debt. 2. To leap or spring: Tess *bounded* for the telephone. **bounded, bounding.**

breath (BRETH) 1. Air taken in and out of the lungs. 2. The moisture or vapor carried out with air from the lungs: On a cold day you can see your *breath.* 3. Power, spirit, life, or time: We'll save our *breath* for the hard work. 4. A rest: Let me take a *breath* before we go on.

bur·row
(BER-oh) 1. A hole or tunnel in the ground, especially one serving as an animal's dwelling: Rabbits  live in *burrows.* 2. Dig a hole in the ground: The mole quickly *burrowed* out of sight. **burrowed, burrowing.**

ce·re·bral pal·sy (sə-REE-brel PAWL-zee *or* SEHR-ə-brel PAWL-zee) Paralysis caused by damage to the brain before or at birth.

char·ac·ter (KA-rik-tər) 1. Moral or spiritual quality; moral strength: It takes *character* to overcome temptation. 2. Person in a play or story.

cin·na·mon (SIN-ə-mən) 1. A reddish-brown spice made from the bark of a tree found in the East Indies. 2. A reddish-brown color.

clan (KLAN) Group of relatives or related families.

clear (KLIHR) 1. Easily seen through: The window was *clear.* 2. To make tidy: *Clear* the dishes from the table. **clearer, clearest, cleared, clearing.**

clump (KLUHMP) 1. A solid mass; a lump: a *clump* of mud. 2. A group of things close together: a *clump* of bushes. 3. A dull thud; the sound of heavy footsteps. **clumped, clumping.**

cock (KOK) To place, wear, or hold in a tilted position: The bird *cocked* its head to one side. **cocked, cocking.**

course (KORSS) 1. A particular way or direction through time: "When in the *course* of human events . . . " (Declaration of Independence). 2. Surely, certainly: Of *course* you can go!

cov·er (KUHV-ər) 1. To put something over or on in order to hide or keep safe: Please *cover* your schoolbooks. 2. To blanket: The leaves *cover* the grass. 3. To dress; put on clothes: *Cover* your head in the rain. 4. Anything that covers, as a lid, a hat, a blanket. **covered, covering.**

crack·le (KRAK-əl) 1. To make sudden, sharp, snapping sounds: The fire *crackled* whenever a dry log was put on it. 2. A sudden sharp sound. **crackled, crackling.**

cra·ter (KRAY-tər) 1. The hollowed-out opening at the top of a volcano. 2. Any cup-like opening formed by nature or by the crash of a meteor or bomb.

cres·cent (KRESS-ənt) 1. The shape of the moon when it is less than a quarter full. 2. Anything of this shape.

cross (KRAWSS) 1. A shape (+) formed by one vertical line cutting across the middle of a horizontal line. 2. To go or pass across: Don't *cross* the street until the light turns green. **crossed, crossing.**

crys·tal (KRISS-tl) 1. A type of glass that is clear. 2. A regularly shaped solid with many definite planes. 3. Clear: *crystal* water.

del·i·cate (DEL-i-kit) 1. Beautifully fine, light, or airy: The bride wore a dress of *delicate* lace. 2. Broken easily; fragile: Eggs are *delicate.*

di·rec·tion (də-REK-shən) 1. The act of advising, guiding, or commanding: Students work under the teacher's *direction.* 2. A line or course followed relative to points on the compass: In what *direction* are you going? 3. Instructions: Follow the *directions* on the bottle.

ex·er·cise (EK-sər-sighz) 1. To move or use the different parts of the body: He *exercises* for ten minutes every day to keep in shape. 2. Practice: You must finish your violin *exercises* before you go out to play. **exercised, exercising.**

fetch (FECH) 1. Go and get; bring: Please *fetch* me my glasses. 2. Cause to come; succeed in bringing: Her call *fetched* me. **fetched, fetching.**

fork 1. A utensil with two or more sharp points used for handling food. 2. Anything shaped like a fork. **forked, forking.**

for·ward (FOR-wərd) 1. At or toward the front: We entered at the *forward* door of the plane. 2. Toward the opponent's goal: He threw a *forward* pass. 3. To send on: Please *forward* the mail to our new address. **forwarded, forwarding.**

fume (FYOOM) 1. To send out unpleasant vapors, odors, gas, or smoke: The fire will *fume* if you don't put it out well. 2. Unpleasant smoke, vapors, gases, or odors. **fumed, fuming.**

gin·ger·bread (JIN-jer-bred) A brown cake flavored with ginger. *Gingerbread* is a good dessert.

gla·cier (GLAY-shər) A large mass of ice, formed from snow that moves slowly down mountain slopes.

gold·en·rod (GOHL-dn-rod) A tall weed with yellow flowers.

gum (GUHM) A sticky juice from trees used for gluing things together; the tree from which it is obtained. **gummed, gumming.**

hail (HAYL) 1. Small, round pieces of ice that fall from the sky like rain: *Hail* fell with such violence that it broke windows. 2. To fall as hail from the sky: a *hail* of bullets.

hand·i·cap (HAN-dee-kap) A disadvantage or drawback, especially a physical one: Deafness is a severe *handicap*. **handicapped, handicapping.**

jam 1. To squeeze or push: *jam* onto the train. 2. To use or push suddenly: He *jammed* on the brakes. **jammed, jamming.**

liq·uid (LIK-wid) 1. Something like water that is able to flow and change into the shape of whatever holds it. 2. Melted: Pour *liquid* butter over the popcorn.

mid·air (MID-air) The middle of the air; the air above the ground: The acrobat made a somersault in *midair*.

nudge (NUHJ) 1. To push against lightly: Tess *nudged* her sister to wake her up. 2. A light push. **nudged, nudging.**

o·be·di·ence (oh-BEE-dee-ənss) Obeying; doing what one is told to do.

or·der (OR-dər) 1. The way in which one thing follows another: numerical *order*. 2. A request for something wanted: Mother phoned her *order* to the grocery store. **ordered, ordering.**

out·line (OWT-lighn) 1. Line that shows the shape of an object: We saw the *outlines* of the mountains against the sky. 2. A general plan; rough draft: Make an *outline* before trying to write a composition.

pelt 1. To hit again and again: The hail *pelted* us. 2. To throw things at. **pelted, pelting.**

perch 1. A place for a bird to sit. 2. To sit, rest, or alight on a particular place. **perched, perching.**

po·lar bear (POH-lər BAIR) A large white bear found in the Arctic or north polar regions.

pol·lute (pə-LOOT) To make impure or tainted. **polluted, polluting.**

pol·lu·tion (pə-LOO-shən) The dirtying of any part of the environment, especially with waste material.

pouch (POWCH) 1. A small bag. 2. A fold that resembles a sack: kangaroo's *pouch.*

prick·ly (PRIK-lee) 1. Having many sharp points or thorns: a *prickly* rosebush. 2. Sharp and stinging: Heat sometimes causes a *prickly* rash on the skin. **pricklier, prickliest.**

prob·a·bly (PROB-ə-blee) more likely than not.

res·cue (RESS-kyoo) 1. To save from danger. 2. Deliverance from danger. **rescued, rescuing.**

res·er·va·tion (rez-ər-VAY-shən) 1. A piece of land set apart by the government for a special use. 2. Something held for a person: Jenny had a *reservation* for a seat at the game.

rheu·ma·tism (ROO-mə-tiz-əm) A disease that affects the muscles and joints with stiffness and pain.

rise (RIGHZ) 1. To move from a lying or a sitting position to a standing position. 2. To get out of bed. 3. Come above the horizon: The sun *rises* in the morning. **rose, risen, rising.**

road·run·ner (ROHD-ruhn-ər) A crested, long-tailed bird of the southwestern United States that is able to run very swiftly.

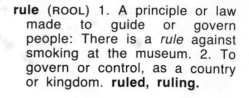

rule (ROOL) 1. A principle or law made to guide or govern people: There is a *rule* against smoking at the museum. 2. To govern or control, as a country or kingdom. **ruled, ruling.**

rus·tle (RUHSS-l) 1. To make a soft, crackling sound like that made by leaves in the wind: Did you hear something *rustle* in the bushes? 2. To steal livestock: The thieves *rustled* 30 cows from the ranch. **rustled, rustling.**

sag 1. To sink or bend. 2. To droop. **sagged, sagging.**

scent (SENT) 1. Odor, smell: Foxes have a strong *scent.* 2. Sense of smell: Hunting dogs must have a sharp *scent.* 3. To smell. The dogs *scent* the deer. **scented, scenting.**

serv·ice sta·tion (SER-viss STAY-shən) A building or place used for fixing automobiles.

sew·age (SOO-ij) The waste carried away by a sewer.

soar (SOR) 1. To fly high without any movement that can be seen; rise upward in the air: The hawk *soars* to a great height. 2. To rise to a higher level than usual: The price of fresh fruit will *soar* this winter. **soared, soaring.**

sol·id (SOL-id) 1. Firm; hard: Some melons were *solid,* but others were soft. 2. Not in the form of liquid or gas: Ice is water in a *solid* form. 3. Not hollow: My candy egg is hollow, but Jan's is *solid* chocolate. 4. Firm and stiff, strong, well-built: The shaky old house was not very *solid.*

spice (SPYSS) 1. A plant with a pleasing, strong smell or taste, used to give a special taste to food. 2. To add spice to. **spiced, spicing, spicy.**

squint (SKWINT) 1. To look with the eyes partly closed. 2. A looking with partly closed eyes. **squinted, squinting.**

straight (STRAYT) 1. Not bent or curved: I can't draw a *straight* line. 2. In a line; in order: The desks were *straight* when class began. 3. Not bending or tipping: Stand *straight.* **straighter, straightest.**

strike (STRIGHK) 1. Hit. 2. To indicate (the time) by making a hitting sound: The clock *strikes* six. 3. To swing the bat at and miss a pitched ball. 4. To make burn by rubbing: *strike* a match. **struck, striking.**

stroke (STROHK) 1. The act or sound of striking. 2. A gentle rubbing with the hand or a brush. **stroked, stroking.**

strug·gle (STRUHG-əl) 1. Make great efforts with the body; try hard: The poor have to *struggle* for a living. 2. Get, move, or make one's way with great effort: The old horse *struggled* to its feet. **struggled, struggling.**

stuff (STUHF) 1. Substance; any material from which something is made. 2. To fill; pack tightly. **stuffed, stuffing.**

sup·pose (sə-POHZ) 1. To assume; imagine or pretend for the sake of argument or to prove a point: *Suppose* the wheel had not been invented. 2. Believe, think, or imagine: I *suppose* he will come at noon. 3. To expect or guess: I *suppose* it will rain today. **supposed, supposing.**

tour (TUR) 1. A personal overall inspection of an area: The children took their parents on a *tour* of the school. 2. A sightseeing trip: a *tour* of Europe. **toured, touring.**

tow·er (TOW-ər) 1. A high, thin building or such a part of a building: The bells are in the church *tower.* 2. To stand high or tall: John and Jan *tower* over Bob. **towered, towering.**

treat (TREET) 1. To act toward; to handle: She *treats* the children with kindness. 2. Something enjoyable. **treated, treating.**

tuft (TUHFT) A small bunch of threads, feathers, hair, or such held together at one end or growing closely together. **tufted, tufting.**

twine (TWIGHN) 1. A strong cord made by twisting many threads together. 2. To twist or weave together. **twined, twining.**

twin·kle (TWING-kəl) 1. To shine or gleam with quick flashes. 2. A quick motion of the eye; wink; blink. **twinkled, twinkling.**

up·right (UHP-right) 1. Vertical; straight: The flagpole should be upright. 2. Vertically; straight up: Stand upright.

va·por (VAY-pər) 1. Smoke or moisture hanging in the air: Fog is water vapor 2. A gas formed by heating a liquid: vapor from a kettle.

wel·come (WEL-kəm) 1. To receive with pleasure: The farmers welcomed the spring rain. 2. A kind or friendly reception: You will always have a welcome here. 3. Free to enjoy courtesies, etc., without obligation (said in response to thanks): You are quite welcome. 4. Exclamation of friendly greeting: Welcome everyone! **welcomed, welcoming.**

wrong (RAWNG) 1. Immoral; unjust; illegal: To beat an animal is wrong. 2. Not correct or true. His answer is wrong. 3. Out of order; not working as it should: Something is wrong with the car.

zig·zag (ZIG-zag) 1. The pattern made by a series of back-and-forth motions with sharp turns and angles. 2. To move with or make many sharp turns: The dogs saw the deer zigzag through the woods. **zigzagged, zigzagging.**